THE
GOLDEN BOOK
OF
COLONIAL CRAFTS

THE GOLDEN BOOK OF COLONIAL CRAFTS

selected from **THE FAMILY CREATIVE WORKSHOP**
created by Plenary Publications International, Inc.

GOLDEN PRESS · NEW YORK

Western Publishing Company, Inc.
Racine, Wisconsin

ALLEN DAVENPORT BRAGDON
Editor-in-Chief and Publisher
of THE FAMILY CREATIVE WORKSHOP.
President, Plenary Publications
International, Incorporated.

NANCY J. JACKSON
Project Editor

Photographs, Colonial Life, taken
at Old Sturbridge Village, Massachusetts.
Folk Art, birth certificate and dower
chest, courtesy of Philadelphia Museum
of Art; weather vane, courtesy of
Creative Art Gallery. Photograph of
old Hires sign, Home Brewing, courtesy
of Hires Division, Crush International, Inc.

The text and illustrations in this book originally appeared in
THE FAMILY CREATIVE WORKSHOP published by Plenary Publications
International, Inc., 300 East 40 Street, New York, New York 10016,
for the Blue Mountain Crafts Council

Printed in the U.S.A.

Library of Congress Catalog Card Number: 74–20158

GOLDEN and GOLDEN PRESS ® are trademarks of
Western Publishing Company, Inc.
THE FAMILY CREATIVE WORKSHOP ® is a trademark of
Plenary Publications International, Inc.

Contents

A Word from the Editors

Many of the contemporary crafts which now enrich our leisure time were, to the Colonists, survival skills, practiced out of necessity. Over three centuries ago, these tough-minded, independent people gave up their familiar lives to try their hand at living in an unknown land. They brought precious little with them except their own abilities, a few tools, and all the ingenuity and inventiveness they could muster. Much of the knowledge that we now think of as crafts enabled them to survive, or supplied whatever small comforts they had in a harsh New World.

For most of us today, life is very different. If we need a tool, we don't have to make it. If we need food, we don't have to plant, water, harvest, and preserve it. If we need clothes, the threads have already been spun and dyed, the cloth woven, cut, and sewn. All kinds of synthetic, man-made materials are available to us in addition to the traditional, natural ones used by the Colonists. Our tools are factory made and electrically powered.

Yet the important things haven't changed. Our hands are as reliable as the Colonists' were. We care about the difference between fine and careless workmanship, and our creative imaginations are no less ingenious than those of 300 years ago. We, too, can learn new skills; we, too, can take pride and satisfaction in creating something beautiful and lasting and unique—something only we could have made. Though we may use different tools and materials, the same craft skills that helped to sustain our Colonial ancestors can enrich our lives in many different ways today.

The projects and activities in this book were selected from hundreds that were originally published in THE FAMILY CREATIVE WORKSHOP, a new, multi-volume encyclopedia of crafts. The skills they teach are typical of our Colonial period, but the editors specify tools, materials, and methods that make sense today. After all, it would be a bit too much to start off an Early American needlework project with instructions to "Plant the flax seeds 16 inches apart!"

Most craft skills and designs used in the Colonial period were passed down from the settlers' European forebears—candlemaking, brewing, musical instruments, needlework, furniture-making. Some were adapted to the materials available here and modified by the demands of a rugged life—folk art, clothing, cornhusk dolls. Many were learned from the native Indians—canoeing, moccasin-making, beadwork, basketry. But they were all passed from person to person. Now, when many of the traditional patterns, techniques, and special know-how our grandparents once learned from their grandparents are no longer being handed down from generation to generation, it is our hope that this book will help to bridge the gap.

There is no substitute for learning how to do something by watching someone who knows how—someone who can share the short-cuts and warn about the tricky parts. The next best thing is a teaching book filled with plenty of photographs and drawings, written by skilled craftspeople. These experienced, practicing artisans, introduced at the beginning of each project, have chosen simple methods to start with, and then show how to progress to more challenging designs, refinements, or variations.

Each craft project is set up like a recipe: all the tools and materials are listed and described at the beginning. The helpful symbols that head every project (see the box below) give a rough indication, in advance, of cost, difficulty, tools, and time required.

Flip through the pages that follow—take a look at the table of contents—run your eye down the index at the back of the book. We hope that you will find projects, craft skills, materials, and ideas that might turn an idle weekend into a penny saved; a gift problem into a loving answer; supply some facts for a social studies assignment; reveal a surprising new twist to a craft skill already well mastered—or maybe even move a vague sense of national pride toward a more real understanding of what it took to survive in an earlier America.

Follow your interest, choose a project, and try it. We will have done our job if you and your family find this book a helpful enough resource to become dog-eared with use in your home.

Allen D. Bragdon

Editor-in-Chief

The Project-Evaluation Symbols appearing in the title heading at the beginning of each project have these meanings:

Range of approximate cost:

¢ Low: under $5 or free and found natural materials

$ Medium: about $10

$$ High: above $15

Estimated time to completion for an unskilled adult:

▨ Hours

🕐 Days

Weeks

Suggested level of experience:

Child alone

Supervised child or family project

Unskilled adult

Specialized prior training

Tools and equipment:
Small hand tools

Large hand and household tools

Specialized or powered equipment

COLONIAL LIFE
Life in Early America

Melissa Schnirring gained her inspiration for this introduction to Colonial life in the early days of rural America during a lengthy stay at the restoration in Sturbridge, Mass. In Old Sturbridge, Colonial life is faithfully recreated in its seasonal rounds by employees hired to carry out the tasks Colonists once pursued. Melissa and her husband, Bill, have a deep interest in the self-reliant life of the rural Colonists and the crafts they ingeniously learned.

Many crafts that we take up today for recreation or as gainful hobbies filled basic needs for the villager-farmer of Colonial America in the late eighteenth and early nineteenth century. A combination of factors left only do-it-yourself or do-without-it alternatives: the isolation often imposed by primitive roads and rough winters, the subsistence (rather than cash crop) farming in remote areas, and the shortage of cash to buy ready-made articles when they were available. It is not easy for today's do-it-yourselfer to grasp the gravity of these alternatives. Truly, sound crafts knowledge made the difference between comfort and bare existence: if you wanted your hands warm during the icy winters, you had to master all the crafts involved in transforming dirty, tangled fleece on a sheep into finished mittens— shearing, carding, spinning, dyeing and knitting.

The New England farmer and his family responded resourcefully to the challenge when the United States was young. They became skilled at handcrafting the articles they needed, using the materials nature provided. Their land was forested, and the trees provided fuel for heating and cooking as well as lumber for buildings, wagons, furniture, barrels, spinning wheels and many other farm and household implements. Trees enriched the family diet by yielding nuts, fruits (for cider and pickling, too) and maple sap for syrup and sugar. The charming little walnut- and apple-face dolls we treasure today were a gift of the forests, too.

In those days the land provided crops that fed the people and their livestock. The livestock in turn gave not only meat, milk, butter and cheese, but wool for clothing, hides for breeches, aprons, caps, boots, buckets, saddles and even drinking mugs, bones for implements, and tallow and grease for candles and soap. The land also furnished herbs for seasoning, flax for clothing, clay for pottery, flowers, leaves, roots, minerals, insects, used for dyeing yarns.

The early Colonists' awareness of nature's bounty and their skill in utilizing it effectively are attributes that we children of technology might well envy today. On the following pages is described a way of life in which crafts played a vital role, filling the pioneers' need for both comfort and creativity. Many of these early crafts—candlemaking, caning, rushing, weaving, cheesemaking, needlework, rug braiding and others—are described in more detail later in the book. For an example of typical life in Colonial America, we have chosen rural New England to show how activities changed with the seasons.

Clothing: Re-enacting life early in the nineteenth century, this Old Sturbridge Village couple (employees of this restoration village) is dressed in Sunday best, ready to attend church or town meeting. Most such clothing was homemade from raw materials prepared by the family. Some items, such as the gentleman's hat, could only be bought in city shops, and were lifelong treasured possessions.

Maple Sugaring: As it was practiced by New England Colonial farmers, maple sugaring is part of the seasonal round in Old Sturbridge Village, Sturbridge, Mass., a museum town that recreates village life in the early days of America. Snow was still on the ground when this first crop of the year, maple sap, was harvested during the early thaws. Note the hollowed logs used to catch the drip, an Indian trick the Colonists learned in the days when buckets were a luxury.

Spinning: This Old Sturbridge Village lady shows how to spin linen yarn from the long inner fibers of the flax plant, gathered on the spindle at the right. The goal is a smooth, even yarn, twisted for strength. Skill is acquired only after much practice.

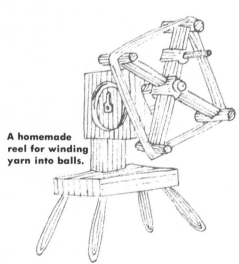

A homemade reel for winding yarn into balls.

For a time fix, we have chosen the period between 1790 and 1840. To evoke scenes from rural America of those years, we photographed in Old Sturbridge Village, Sturbridge, Mass. The Village, open to the public, recreates village and farm life of this period. Its inhabitants are paid employees, trained in the early farming and craft techniques.

A Look into the Past

As the first half century of the Republic unfolded, the inland rural New England family was an industrious, nearly self-sufficient unit. Of its three main preoccupations (food, clothing and housing), only clothing was not governed by the seasons. Clothmaking was a year-round craft.

Farm life was hard on clothes, almost all of which had to be made at home. A ripped garment meant for a woman one more mending chore that night by the light of the fire or by a burning pine or hemlock knot or tow-wick candle. Nothing that could be repaired was ever discarded. What was worn out became part of something else—an appliqued quilt or a braided rug, for instance, or a patchwork pillow. The constant need for production didn't keep the women from adding touches of grace to their needlework. While not a scrap of cloth could be wasted, simple patchwork, pieced and appliqued, gradually evolved into a folk art of extraordinary originality and beauty.

Babies came along to add to the family's need for cloth, but as they grew, they added hands to fashion it, too. Girls learned to knit with homespun yarns when they were about four years old, to spin homegrown flax into linen thread when they were six. Men, women, and children wove cloth on looms. Boys even took small looms along when they pastured the sheep, weaving while they watched over the herd. From the wool and linen cloth, the women sewed clothes and produced the quilts, rugs, towels, curtains, napkins, and other articles for the home.

Weaving: A year-round task that fell to Colonial women was weaving from farm-grown flax clothing and such items as napkins and table scarfs shown in foreground.

Plowing: Today's Old Sturbridge Village farmers show how to plow with oxen, as did our ancestors. Oxen could keep their footing on New England's rocky, rough slopes and in half-drained swales. They were also used for hauling, stump pulling, other heavy work.

The family managed to combine sociability with cloth production. Women took their spinning wheels when they visited neighbors and they organized the quilting and spinning bees that whiled away the hours that could be spared from the year's round of farming activities.

Spring

For the majority of the family's activities, the seasons called the tune in early rural America. Late winter or early spring when the sap rose, was the time for making maple syrup and sugar—although a capricious January thaw could send a farmer out through deep snowdrifts to tap his maples. The Indians, whose generosity in helping the early settlers is rarely acknowledged, had taught the farmers to cut V-shape slashes low on the tree trunks and insert a piece of birch bark in each slash to funnel the sap. The farmers improved on this, if a hand auger was available, by drilling into the trunk and replacing the birch bark with a hollow tube.

Spring was also the time for sheep shearing and much of the planting. New England farms were 50 to 200 acres in size at this time, but only half a dozen of these acres on each would be in crops at one time, with perhaps twice that much in meadows or in partly cleared permanent pasture for swine and cattle. With the primitive implements available around 1800, it was a very hard day's work to plow an acre and even slower, backbreaking labor to harvest it. A farmer thought twice before he planted additional acreage, especially if he didn't have a ready market for the surplus—that is, if he didn't live near a sizable town or at least close to a river, by far the best means of transportation in those days.

Maize (Indian corn) was the basic crop and the basic foodstuff for farm families and, along with hay, for livestock winter feed. Hard work breeds hearty appetites, but our educated palates today would surely rebel at such an incessant onslaught of corn: corn mush (hasty pudding), boiled corn, roasted corn, corn meal baked into corn cake and corn pudding. (And the husks made cornhusk dolls!) A blight of parasites harbored in barberry bushes had wiped out wheat crops by 1800 in all New England except Vermont and along the western borders. This meant the virtual disappearance of white bread; the substitute was corn meal and rye flour bread called "rye and Injun."

Churning Butter: It required little skill but lots of elbow grease to keep the wooden handle moving up and down until the butter solidified. Churning was one of the many chores that kept housewives busy throughout the year.

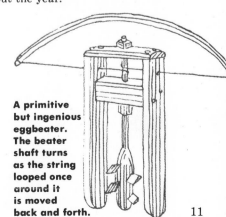

A primitive but ingenious eggbeater. The beater shaft turns as the string looped once around it is moved back and forth.

Haying: Lacking mechanical aids such as mowers and balers, the early American harvested hay for his livestock by hand, using hand-made implements.

A homemade wooden fork for pitching hay

Candle Dipping: Simple but time-consuming, the making of candles by hand was best done outdoors because it was a messy, smelly chore done over an open fire. The number of dips determined the candles' size and lasting power.

Besides corn, the farmer planted hay, together with a shade crop of oats, in the spring. (The hay would not be ready for harvest until the following year, but the oats would be ready in August.) He also planted flax to provide the fibers from which the women spun thread for the weaving of cloth. Potatoes and the kitchen garden (including most of the vegetables we know today except for the tomato) went in as soon as the earth warmed, along with herbs, destined for the meat stews that would provide some variation from the eternal diet of corn. Throughout the growing season, as each crop ripened, there would be preserving and pickling chores for the women and girls, as well as jams to make to stock the larder against winter.

Summer

The frantic pace of the spring planting season eased a little as the weather warmed. Though there were hay, rye, and oats to be harvested and potatoes for everyone to help dig, other chores sent the family ranging the countryside, and these were more like diversions. Fishing was a legitimate chore, and snaring added to the variety summer brought to meals. In the hot, lazy days of midsummer, there were berries to gather, first raspberries and wild strawberries, then blueberries. There were sweet-smelling herbs to seek, for strewing on the church benches and for making little dried nosegays to scent drawers and linen stores. Other herbs were for medicinal uses, and other berries, nuts, and barks (maple, walnut, and oak) for the dyeing of yarns.

For the farmer, as the kitchen garden grew, there was the special joy of watching over, nurturing, harvesting, and drying the seeds of those vegetables that were the best of the year's crop, to provide good seed for the next year's sowing. As the season waxed, then waned, the family began to collect the materials that made the winter months' craft production possible —the right piece of wood to carve a toy, a staircase railing, or a spindle;

perhaps special boards to bend and smooth for a cradle for the baby to come, rushes for winter basketmaking, a gnarled brier root for a pipe, stalks of broomcorn for a new broom.

Summer was the time for home improvement on a large scale. These were the years when rural New Englanders were beginning to turn their log cabins into buildings for livestock and were constructing frame houses for their families. In more remote areas, they still hewed the beams (oak in New York, maple in Vermont, chestnut elsewhere if it was more plentiful) and sawed the boards by hand (white pine for flooring and siding), but sawmills now began to appear on every New England river. A nailmaking machine had been invented, so nails were no longer rare and expensive. After weeks (with a sawmill nearby) or months of preparation, neighbors were summoned to help join and raise the frame for the new house. This was always a festive occasion, with outdoor tables groaning with food and drink prepared by the new home owners for all the helping hands.

All was not unrelieved toil for the farm family, especially as the nineteenth century progressed. Depending on the severity of the customs of the district, there was fun to be had. Bees were organized for men as well as women—to clear a field of stumps, to raise a house, to augment a farmer's lumber supply, and, most popular of all, to husk maize. After a cornhusking, there was always time for athletic contests. Hunting, fishing, skating and swimming in season were popular with men. There were Training Day with its public shooting matches (later replaced by Independence Day), boisterous Election Day, County Court Day, and the agricultural fairs of the early 1800s.

Fall

With autumn came the last urgent preparations for the months ahead, when the land would lie still under its winter blanket, and warmth and food would depend on the industry and wisdom of the preceding seasons. There was corn to be harvested, rye for the following year to be sown. The last of the fruits and vegetables had to be picked and stored, dried or pickled, or preserved.

The men did the heaviest work, but for the women it was a time of almost frenzied activity. The fall crop of apples had to be sliced and hung on long strings from the rafters to dry, or else stored in barrels in the cellar, straw separating the layers to avoid that one bad apple that could spoil the lot. The last of the garden crops were stored—potatoes, turnips, onions, beets, cabbage, parsnips, carrots, squash, pumpkins, pears, whatever would keep.

Autumn brought butchering time, and for a few weeks there was fresh meat. Most of it had to be pickled in brine, though some of it was smoked or dried, for future use. Animal fat was rendered into tallow for candles, which had to be made outdoors. The women raced against time to prepare a good supply while the fair weather (Indian summer, if they were fortunate) lasted. They slipknotted candlewicks onto candle rods and dipped them, with intervals for cooling, as many as 40 times into the tallow in a large iron cauldron over an open fire. They also used animal fat for soapmaking, combining it with lye from leached ashes. Some dyeing had to be done in the fall, too, yellow from goldenrod or onions, for example.

The men threshed the harvested rye on the barn floor with a flail, separating the grain from the straw, then winnowed it outdoors in a shallow bowl, tossing the grain in the air so the wind could blow away the chaff. Silage corn for the livestock was cut and stored in September. Corn intended for human consumption was tied in bunches or shocks and left in the fields to dry and harden. Later on, some of it was brought in, husked, shelled (in some cases with a flail, but usually with a knife or crank-operated corn sheller), and taken to the nearest mill for grinding into corn meal. Some shocks were left in the fields until needed in winter.

Winter

Once the flying snows of winter had locked in the last pasture, important indoor tasks were waiting: the ever-present cloth production; repairing or

Broommaking: With the aid of this primitive but efficient binding machine, the Colonial broommaker could produce ten or twelve sturdy brooms in an hour.

A Colonial broom made of broomcorn stalks.

making tools, implements, and furniture; mending boots and shoes (more likely the former—the virgin forest and mossy topsoil, now eroded, held moisture like a sponge, and the farmer almost always wore boots); repairing harnesses; lacing together cracked or broken pottery with linen thread; and, as spring approached, husking and shelling corn (always the best ears with the straightest rows of kernels were set aside for planting) and threshing grain for the coming sowing.

But the farm family was by no means locked in. Quite the opposite. The snows smoothed the primitive roads and made sleighing parties feasible, trips to town easier (some towns even used rollers to pack down the road snow) and visits to distant friends possible. Families packed and came to stay for days and perhaps for weeks, catching up on all that had happened since the previous year. And even if they stayed at home, there was time during the frozen months for a man to carve that brier pipe, for a woman to cross-stitch a sampler, for a daughter to augment her hope chest.

The snow also opened the way for a chore that rivaled cloth production for

Blacksmithing: Old Sturbridge Village's faithful reproduction of a Colonial blacksmith's shop includes a lever-operated, overhead bellows and the wide variety of tongs and other tools needed for forging and tempering metal.

Log Splitting: Colonial farmers often split logs for boardmaking by hand, but they took advantage of any available riverside sawmills to cut wood for houses, barns, fences, tools, and furniture.

its absolute necessity: getting in firewood for the year. Farm life required firewood in awesome quantities. The kitchen fireplace or stove was always wood hungry. In a large house, a fireplace or stove in the parlor used wood in winter. Dyeing, soapmaking and the smokehouse consumed a lot of wood in autumn. And in season, maple sugaring created a tremendous demand, since the farmer had to boil down 35 to 40 gallons of the maple sap to get one gallon of maple syrup. With further boiling, he got about eight pounds of maple sugar from one gallon of syrup. In the early 1800s, a hundred-acre farm often produced as much as 1,000 pounds of sugar a year.

Wood was cut in winter because the task was easier then, on both man and beast. The snow cover made hauling lighter because there was less drag on the sled runners. (Sleds were used for year-round hauling, due to the shortage and expense of wheels.) At first, farmers used a broadax for the cutting of wood and, later on, a two-man saw (no doubt reflecting on the wisdom of the saying that wood was the fuel that warmed you twice, once when you cut it and

Tinsmithing: A tinsmith solders together cut tin pieces, then forms them with hand tools, just as the Colonists did. Early tinsmiths not only produced table and storage vessels, but mended them.

once when you burned it). Frozen wood split more easily, too, and wood cut when the sap wasn't running was less prone to insect attack and more secure for building.

Do-It-Yourself to Fix-It-Yourself

The intense round of seasonal activities on which comfort and even survival depended did not ease as the nineteenth century progressed, but the rural New England farmer's means of coping with them did. In 1790, he was quite likely to make his own boots, hammer out spades and two-tined forks on his own anvil and make whatever new furniture was required. The combined efforts of the men and women produced everything they needed except coffee, tea, spices, molasses, salt and sugar; of these, only salt was indispensable. The local store carried these commodities, in addition to fancier forms of dry goods than the women could make from wool and flax. The farmer could pay for his purchases in cash if he had it or exchange surplus he had produced: cheeses, grain, flaxseed, hides, tallow, lumber, pork, beef, wood ashes.

By the turn of the century, however, peddlers began to carry all sorts of wares to the most remote districts. Visits by traveling artisans became frequent enough to take care of many chores, such as hide tanning and bootmaking. As towns grew larger, more specialized shops appeared: a West India goods store, a hardware store, an apothecary shop, and even a millinery shop. Artisans opened shops: blacksmiths, potters, broommakers, pewterers, coopers, cabinetmakers, and tinsmiths, usually part-time farmers themselves.

Basic materials became more plentiful. Iron mines and blast furnaces, up and down the Connecticut River and along the New York-Massachusetts border, were catching up to the demand, and by 1812, there were 160 cotton mills in the tristate area of Connecticut, Rhode Island and Massachusetts.

By 1840, the degree of craft-dependent self-sufficiency required for survival had diminished, but some of the crafts continued to flourish. And some of the products of necessity that the New England farm families crafted (exquisitely appliqued quilts, for example) not only have survived but are on display in museums today.

Pewtermaking: Old Sturbridge Village pewterer heats a spoon mold over a candle. He will pour in the molten pewter, let it cool, strike it loose, smooth and polish it.

Sheep is placed upright, all four legs extended, to keep it still while it is being sheared. Once seated, animal behaves surprisingly well.

Sheep Shearing and Wool Carding

A review of the early steps in the home production of wool yarns shows some of the effort required in Colonial times to provide raw materials for the craftsman. The process of yarnmaking begins with sheep shearing, a painless—to the sheep— but messy job. The process, by the way, has changed little, although today electric shears are used instead of hand shears.

The shearer placed the sheep upright to immobilize it and began shearing at the neck, working down the underside a distance, then cutting up around the neck and head. So he could roll the fleece back as he worked, he pulled the fleece apart along the center of the underside. Working from the underside up around to the back, he sheared from head to tail, rolling the fleece back as he went and being careful not to cut into the roll, which would mean shortened, useless fibers. A similar pulling-apart process was also necessary for each leg, but the result was an entire, intact fleece. It took an hour or more to shear a sheep with the hand clippers used around 1800, and by the end, the shearer's clothing was covered with the lanolin from the sheep's skin.

Preparing the Wool

The oily wool was cleansed in a large kettle in a mixture of one part urine (usually human; urine was one of the few sources of ammonia then) to two parts water. After being rinsed and dried, it was ready for carding. In Colonial villages, carding was done by hand, at home. The wool had to be picked over to remove bits of dirt, burrs, twigs, and other foreign matter. Then a bit of oil was added to it, and the wool was carefully combed or carded by hand with wooden cards, implements that look like wire brushes. (These can be bought today at craft and hobby shops.) By means of the bristles on the cards, the carder opened the wool fibers, then drew them together, combing the wool from one card to the other, forming at last a roll of fluffy strands (see photograph on opposite page). The wool fibers were then ready for spinning into yarn and dyeing.

Dyeing the Yarn

Before the mid-nineteenth century, basic dyeing was done with such natural substances as dried insects, powdered minerals, roots, flowers, and leaves. When easy-to-use chemical dyes were invented, homemade natural dyestuffs quickly lost popularity. However, a characteristic of natural dyes—the unpredictability of their color—is exactly what makes them appealing to today's home dyers. They produce individual rather than standardized effects on yarn or fabric. No two dye lots are identical.

Some of the natural dye sources that have been used at one period or another can be found in almost every region of the country. Reds and pinks of various shades were obtained from the juices of cherries, strawberries

Old Sturbridge Village shearer demonstrates use of hand shearer, the tool used in Colonial times. Today, shearing is done with electric clippers.

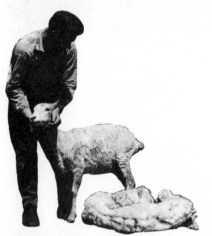

Shorn, the sheep is content to be rid of the hot coat of wool for the summer. The large, intact fleece will be spread out for sorting.

and red raspberries. A reddish purple was made from the berries of common pokeweed. The stalks of sorrel, cardinal flower, red oak and hemlock were also used as sources for reds with a brownish cast. Purple colors were extracted from the juices of wild grapes and wild blueberries. Willow and birch bark were boiled to make rose in a tannish shade, and certain yellows were obtained from willow leaves, marsh marigold, ash bark, tulip tree leaves, ragweed and burdock.

An attractive gold-gray color was obtained by the Colonists from goldenrod. One and a half pecks of goldenrod blossoms, cut near the tops of the stems, were gathered for dyeing one pound of yarn. The blossoms were soaked overnight in water in a large kettle. Next day, they were boiled in water for two hours. After cooling, the mixture was strained through several layers of cheesecloth. On the third day, it was ready to be used for the dye bath.

Other yellow shades were obtained from various other flowers and from dried onion skins. More than half of the natural dyes produced yellows. Browns were obtained from black-walnut hulls and various barks, rusts from madder and other roots, green-grays from many plants, including bayberry, lily-of-the-valley leaves, and sedges. The indigo peddler supplied the blues.

The first step in the dyeing process was mordanting the spun-yarn fibers.

This prepared them to receive the dye, combine with it and form an insoluble compound, thus fixing the color. The Colonists used a mixture of potash alum and cream of tartar or, after 1820, a chrome mordant, all obtainable from village stores. Two huge kettles were suspended over open fires. One held plain water, in which the yarn was presoaked for about an hour; in the other was the warm mordant bath. After soaking, the yarn was transferred to the mordant bath, left for an hour over the fire, then allowed to cool gradually, removed, rinsed in cool water, and hung to dry.

For the dyeing, a large kettle was filled with water and another with four to five gallons of the strained color mixture. As in the mordanting process, the yarn had an hour's presoak in hot water; then it spent an hour in the dye bath, kept just below the boiling point. For rinsing, the yarn went back to the hot-water kettle, and cold water was gradually added until the water was cold. The yarn was then hung to dry.

You can use these same processes today for home dyeing. Search out the

Carding: Two cards, each covered with nail-like teeth, were employed to work pieces of sheared fleece into long rolls of wool fibers. The process eliminated short, unworkable fibers, left the others parallel.

Dyeing: Hanks of yarn spun from carded wool were dyed, then hung to dry. Wool dyeing, like candle dipping, was done outdoors because both generated unpleasant odors.

Wool was placed on one card and brushed lightly with the other until spread evenly. Heavier strokes were then used to return it to the other card, and the process was repeated—and repeated.

natural dye materials in season because the purest colors result from using fresh flower or plant material picked just as it is reaching maturity. Strict adherence to mordanting and dyeing times and temperatures are also required for purity of color. Avoid hard water, which would cause the dye to spot and be irregularly distributed, as would crowding the material in the bath. Finally, the dye kettle itself can affect the colors, "saddening" (dulling) or brightening them: iron kettles tend to dull colors; copper kettles give a brighter color result and brass kettles produce even brighter color. Enameled kettles do not affect color.

Dyeing with natural materials, as the Colonists did produced the subtle, gentle, earthy tones we associate with paintings of the period, and is a fascinating exercise for the modern craftsman. The dyes held well and rarely faded. Although somewhat unpredictable, the colors are appropriate for homespuns and handwoven fabrics. Materials for home dyeing are readily available and easily improvised.

The following pages give detailed step-by-step instructions for many traditional early American crafts that were practiced by our Colonial ancestors, but using materials and supplies available today.

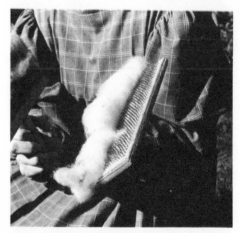

After many repetitions, the wool was at last a light and fluffy roll, ready for spinning into yarn, the next step in the long transition from curly fleece to items such as clothing, blankets and rugs.

Ancient and Modern

Shirlee Saunders Isaacson has been associated with schools and teaching most of her adult life. Her interest in the crafts began with the instruction of young people. An expert in many craft areas, Shirlee is now associated with a crafts boutique near her Roslyn, L. I. home.

Basket making is not only one of man's oldest crafts, but one of the most universal. From Iraq to Egypt and from Europe to China, ancient basket makers were practicing their expertise long before recorded history. The Indians of this continent have been skilled basket weavers for at least 9,000 years and are considered to be among the world's most talented basket making peoples.

It is impossible to trace basketry back through time to its earliest roots because the natural-fiber materials used then, and now, are perishable. It is known, however, that basketry preceded pottery as a craft in both North and South America. Coiled baskets, described on page 21, were probably the first baskets constructed by prehistoric man.

Basket making materials are readily available and inexpensive. A one-pound hank of round cane, for instance, is about the price of two pounds of butter. The techniques of basket making are easy to master.

Glossary of terms

Hank: A one pound bundle. Basketry materials are sold by the hank.

Base: Bottom of the basket. Baskets generally are woven from the base up.

Wooden base: A flat piece of wood with holes into which are set stakes (see below) on which the basket sides are woven. See page 22 for an example of a wooden base.

Woven base: Stakes interwoven to form basket base. See page 24, photographs 16, 17 and 18.

Footing: A row of weaving worked around the base when a wooden base is used. See page 22 for an example, photograph 10.

Stakes: The canes used to make a woven base; also, those set into a base to create the framework on which the basket sides are woven.

Upsetting: Term to describe the setting of stakes into a base to form uprights on which sides are woven. These are called "upsett stakes."

Weavers: Cane, or other basketry materials, with which the sides and sometimes the base are woven.

Piecing weavers: Term used to describe the technique for working a new weaver into the basket when the previous weaver is used up. The new weaver is placed behind the stake where the previous weaver ended. Basketry materials are dampened before using to make them supple; when the basket is completed, the weavers dry and become rigid so weaver ends stay where placed. (Clip ends when basket is finished, inside, close to weaving.)

Simple weaving: Technique in which a single weaver is passed over one stake and under the next. In simple weaving, an odd number of stakes must be used. The pencil holder project, page 20, is an example of simple weaving.

Pairing: Technique in which two weavers are intertwined around each stake, then woven, one in front, one behind, each stake. See page 24, photograph 19.

Double pairing: Pairing worked with two pairs (four) weavers. Two go behind the stakes, two in front. See page 24, photograph 20.

Triple weaving: Similar to pairing, but three weavers are used, or three pairs of weavers. The bottom weaver always goes over the top weaver, so weavers are intertwined as they entwine stakes. See photograph 12, page 22, and figure B, page 22.

Waling: A strip of braided weavers, two or more, used to accent and strengthen basket work. See photographs 21 and 22, page 25.

This shopping basket offers a challenge to the basket maker because it combines three weaving techniques. Instructions for making it begin on page 24.

Pencil holder

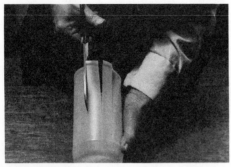

1: With scissors, make 13 cuts, 4½ inches deep, in a 1-quart plastic bottle from which the neck and the shoulders have been removed.

2: Weave yarn in and out of stakes, starting with end inside bottle. Weave five rounds aqua, five black, 16 green, four black. Attach colors by knotting ends.

3: With scissors, round off plastic stake ends about 1 inch above the last row of weaving, which is looped and knotted.

This project helps the beginner in basketry to understand simple weaving, a technique basic to basket making. The basket base here is made from a 1-quart plastic bottle with sides cut to create 13 stakes. Instead of cane weavers, you work with heavy knitting worsted, 2½ yards of aqua, three of black, seven of green. To turn the bottle into a pencil holder, follow photographs 1 through 3. Sketches below show how to finish off the last row. Work figure A around each stake, draw the yarn inside the holder, knot the yarn, cut. Work yarn ends into the weaving.

To understand basic basket weaving techniques, try this easy beginner's project, fashioning a pencil holder from worsted knitting yarn and a one-quart plastic bottle.

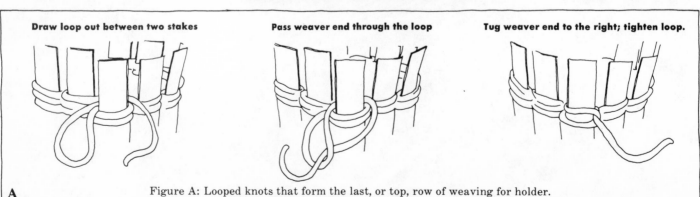

Draw loop out between two stakes   **Pass weaver end through the loop**   **Tug weaver end to the right; tighten loop.**

A   Figure A: Looped knots that form the last, or top, row of weaving for holder.

Indian coil basket

With natural reeds and grasses, American Indians coiled storage containers for food and made a variety of useful objects, including sleeping mats and large shallow baskets, which, pitch-coated, were used as boats.

To make coil baskets, you can use grass or bundles of dry pine needles for the core and rush or marsh grass for wrapping. Gather rush in early spring, when it can be split while green and tender. Green materials shrink, so they must be dried before they can be used. For green-gray hues, dry the split rush in the shade. For brown and tan highlights, dry it in the sun. Dry grasses for about a week—pine needles even longer.

Before you attempt to make coil baskets with plant materials, practice with this easy version, using yarn for wrapping and rope for the core. Materials are about one skein each of blue and white knitting worsted; 20 feet of ½-inch rope; a tapestry needle; scissors.

Starting the base: With blue yarn threaded through the tapestry needle, stitch through the rope to make the first coil, as in photograph 4. Wind the yarn around and around the rope until an inch or so is covered.

Joining coils: Coil this yarn-wrapped inch around the beginning end, and join the two coils by looping the yarn back over the first coil twice. Change colors, as in photograph 5. Wrap an inch of rope in white, loop a joining stitch back over the previous coil. Continue wrapping and joining until a white coil has circled the blue coil. Repeat, making joining stitches at every inch point, and changing colors as each coil is circled.

Making the base: Coil and join eight rounds, side by side.

Making the sides: Coil and join five rounds, one on top of the other.

Making the handles: As you work the fifth side round, make handles by skipping joining stitches for a 6-inch span on both sides of the coil: Raised, the yarn-wrapped spans become handles.

Rope and yarn make up the core and the wrapping for this coiled basket. Indian craftsmen used dry pine needles or grass for the core, rush or marsh grass for wrapping.

4: To form first coil, yarn is stitched through rope end twice, at points ¾ inch apart, then drawn tight.

5: One-inch tail of new yarn is stitched through previous yarn, then drawn forward with tail of old yarn, and wrapped.

6: Joining stitches show here as spokes of contrasting color looped back over previous coil. Make two loops at each point.

7: Basket base is made of eight rounds, coiled side by side: Five more coils, one on top of the other, form sides.

8: Basket handles are formed in top coil by leaving six yarn-wrapped spans unjoined. Raised spans become handles.

21

Hanging basket

Handcrafted baskets woven of natural cane are remarkably sturdy. In many countries, cane basketry is still used to produce strong travel cases and saddle packs for horses and donkeys. Natural cane is used here to make a hanging basket holder for a plant.

Materials needed are one hank of No. 2 round cane for weavers and chain links; 25 10-inch stakes of No. 4 round cane; a 6-inch wooden base of 3/16-inch plywood (sold in craft shops), in which 25 holes ½ inch from the edge have been made with a ⅛-inch drill bit; needle-nose pliers. Before you begin, study these rules for working with cane.

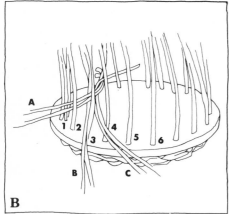

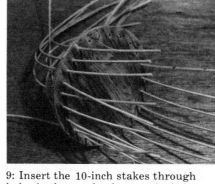

Figure B: The triple weaving of sides for the plant holder basket begins with the placement of three pairs of weavers, ends twisted together, inside a framework of upsett stakes. Insert two strands of weaver A between stakes 1 and 2; two strands of weaver B between stakes 2 and 3; two strands of weaver C between stakes 3 and 4. Starting with weaver A, pass A over weavers B and C, in front of stake 2, then back of stake 3 and pull it out in front of stake 4; then pass B over C and A, in front of stake 3, back of 4, pull it out in front of 5; then pass weaver C over A and B, in front of stake 4, back of stake 5, and pull it out in front of stake 6 (photograph 12). Repeat these steps until triple weaving is completed, then clip weaver ends to one inch lengths, and tuck them inside the weaving in the interior of the basket sides.

9: Insert the 10-inch stakes through holes in the wooden base, ½ inch from the edge. Footing is woven of 4-inch stake ends protruding from bottom of base.

10: Footing is woven with basket base facing you. Pass each stake end through next three stakes, counterclockwise, under, over, under—last three into first loops.

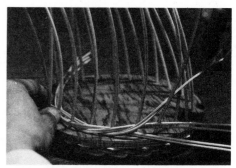

11: Turn the base sideways to snug the footing to the base, gently pulling the six-inch side stakes toward the base. Set basket upright to work woven sides.

12: View of the beginning of triple weave pattern, detailed in figure B. Three pairs of weavers are used here. Note that bottom weaver always goes over the top weaver.

13: Footing pattern in photograph 10 is repeated with tops of side canes to form basket rim, but weaving is looser and is worked clockwise.

14: Scissors are used to trim to ¼ inch all cane ends protruding from the basket rim and base, and those created when joining weavers were worked into sides.

Because a hanging basket must be strong enough to support the weight of a potted plant, it is best constructed with triple-woven cane on a wooden base.

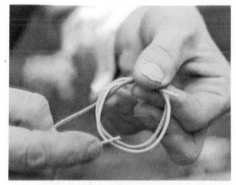

15: Links for the basket chain are made of well-moistened 18-inch weavers cut from No. 2 round cane. First link of each nine-link chain, is made by forming a 1½ inch circle at one end of the weaver, and weaving the other end back through this circle until three rounds are closely intertwined. Form the next link through the first, and repeat until nine links are joined. Make three chains, and attach them at the top with a single link, woven through the last link in each chain.

Working with natural cane: There are four important rules to remember:
□ Cane that is to be woven, pinched, or bent, must be soaked for half an hour before using, or it may crack while you are working.
□ Keep cane moist while you work by covering it with a damp towel.
□ Work with weavers of manageable length. Mine are under 4 feet.
□ Guide weavers gently and place, never yank or pull, between stakes.

Making the footing: Hold the wooden base firmly and pull each of the 25 10-inch stakes through one of the holes in the base, leaving about six inches on top, four on the bottom, as in photograph 9. Weave these bottom-of-the-base cane tips to create the footing, as in photograph 10. Use the pliers to pinch and bend the cane if it is stiff. These maneuvers are standard when making a basket with a wooden base.

Triple-weaving the sides: Turn the base sideways and snug the footing to the base by pulling gently on the top stakes. Turn base right side up, and triple weave for ten rounds around the vertical stakes, working with three pairs of weavers of No. 2 cane cut in 4-foot lengths. See Figure B.

Making the rim: When sides are complete, make the rim by repeating the footing pattern, photograph 13, with the tops of the vertical stakes.

Attaching the chains: Three chains of cane links, shown in photograph 15, are attached to basket sides by weaving the last link of each chain through a loop in the footing row on top of the basket.

Shopping basket

To make the shopping basket shown in color on page 19, you will need 31 16-inch stakes of No. 4 round cane for the sides; six 20-inch stakes and nine 10-inch stakes of No. 4 round cane for the base; a hank of No. 2 round cane for the weavers; round-nosed pliers for pinching stakes before bending. Review the rules for working with natural cane, outlined on page 23.

Starting the woven base: The first step is to tie together with wire, or string, the six 20-inch stakes at a point 6 inches from one end. Divide these six starter stakes into three pairs. Insert through them at the long end, the nine 10-inch cross stakes, as shown in photograph 16. Insert the first close to the tie and center, then space the rest about an inch apart, centering each. Around this 8-inch grid, starting at the tied end, weave 24 rounds of pairing, working with pairs of No. 2 cane in 4-foot lengths, as depicted in photographs 17 and 18.

Adding vertical stakes: The next step is to insert the vertical stakes on which the sides will be woven. Use sharp scissors to cut a tapering end on each of the 31 16-inch stakes. Insert the tapered end of each of these stakes into one of the 30 tunnels formed when you paired around the

16: Tied ends of starter stakes with two cross stakes, the first laced over, under, over; the second under, over, under. Place the seven remaining cross stakes, alternating the weaving pattern. Work the starter stakes in twos.

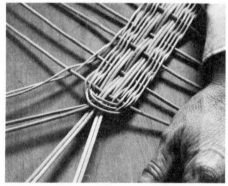

17: Weaving paired canes around stakes. Canes are twined around each other before entwining next stake. For three rounds, weave around each cross stake, but weave over all of the starter stakes as though they were a single unit.

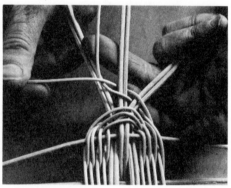

18: Separate the starter stakes into twos again, untie, work three more rounds of pairing, treating each of the three starter-stake twos as a unit this time. Separate the twos into singles; then pair for 18 complete rounds.

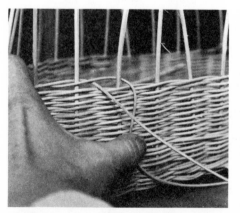

19: Weaving paired canes around basket sides after upsett stakes have been added to base. Pair 24 rounds, working two 4-foot lengths of No. 2 cane. Place weavers gently; never tug or pull them as you work.

20: Double pairing, working with two pairs of weavers instead of with two individual weavers. A single round of double pairing is worked after the 24 rounds of pairing have been completed on basket sides.

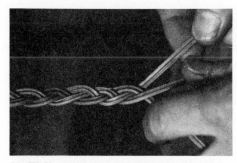

21: Waling, prepared in advance, is used as a single weaver and is made by braiding two or more weavers, or pairs of weavers. Waling that makes sides of this shopping basket is made by braiding three pairs.

22: Simple weave, used to work basket sides with waling, requires odd number of stakes and that's why you add the 31st upsett stake to the basket base. Weave waling in and out of stakes for 16 rounds.

starter stakes. Place the 31st stake in a center, back tunnel. This odd stake, the second in that tunnel, allows you to simple-weave the waling which forms the basket's top.

Finishing the basket bottom: Weave the protruding ends of the six starter stakes and the nine cross stakes—these ends are 3 to 4 inches long now—into the woven base by passing each, counter clockwise, over the two nearest upsett stakes and behind the third. Cut off ends.

The sides: With pliers, pinch, then bend, upsett stakes into vertical position to make framework for sides. Around this framework, with two 4-foot weavers of No. 2 cane, pair 24 rounds, then double pair one round with 4-foot weavers of No. 2 cane, photographs 19 and 20. Simple-weave 16 rounds of prepared waling, photographs 21 and 22. You will have to prepare 40 feet of waling. Follow waling rounds with two rounds of double pairing.

Finishing the basket: About 5 inches of side stake will remain after side weaving is completed. Weave these ends clockwise into a rim, working the weavers as for footing, photograph 10 and photograph 23 on this page. To make basket handles, cut two 5-foot lengths of No. 2 round cane and weave each into a ring 6 inches in diameter, using the technique for making links described on page 23. Attach each round to a basket side with a 14-inch length of No. 4 round cane. Pass the cane behind two stakes inside the basket, poke each end out through the side, as in photograph 24, loop each twice around handle, then around the nearest stake. Singe off frizzles that appear after cane dries.

25: With a lighted match singe off frizzles that appear once the cane has dried, to give the basket a professional finish. Work quickly, or you may find you have set the basket on fire.

23: Footing weave, worked clockwise, is used to make rim of basket from the five inches remaining at the top of the upsett stakes after sides are woven. Weave last three stakes into existing loops.

24: Ends of each cane tie used to attach basket handle are pushed out through basket side, looped twice around handle, and secured to nearest stake. Ends go inside, then are snipped off.

Dip, Cast, Decorate

Anita Wharton, a commercial artist for Lebhar Freidman Incorporated, is also a free-lance photographer and amateur oil painter. She began making candles as a hobby, under the tutelage of a friend. Her hobby grew into a business, and she has sold many candles at art exhibits and craft fairs.

Candlemaking requires a minimum of skill and is something anyone can do, including children, provided they are well supervised. Materials for making candles are available at hobby shops. The type of wax sold at supermarkets—paraffin for sealing preserve jars—makes acceptable candles, and for convenience I use it in the children's project below, but it costs more and is not as good as standard candle wax. For really good candles, buy slabs of white, ready-to-use commercial wax at a hobby shop. Experience will teach you how much wax is needed for a given candle, but as a general guide, a ten-pound slab of raw wax will make four quart-size candles.

Candlewicks are made of braided cotton yarn that has been treated and coated with a thin layer of wax. They are sold in lengths cut from spools and in two or three widths—medium for the average candle, extra thin and extra thick for candles in special sizes.

Stearic acid, an optional wax additive commonly used in making candles, is sold in granule form at hobby shops. It makes wax more opaque, stronger in color, and slower burning. It is added after the wax has been melted. The correct proportion is 20 percent by weight.

Scent oils, added just before the candles are poured into molds, is another optional additive. The fragrance is especially strong immediately after a scented candle has been snuffed out. Bayberry— especially appropriate for Christmas candles—and other essences formulated specifically for wax, such as pine and sandalwood, are sold at many hobby shops. If unavailable locally, you can order from Berje, 43-10 23rd Street, Long Island City, N.Y. 11101.

Wax is flammable, so it is essential that you take every precaution when you are melting it. Use a double boiler; most wax melts at between 110 and 200 degrees Fahrenheit, and a double boiler will keep its temperature from exceeding the boiling point of water (212 degrees Fahrenheit). Never leave melted wax over an open flame unattended, and don't pour or cast it near an open flame. To extinguish wax fires, always keep powdered baking soda handy. Don't use water to extinguish a wax fire should one occur.

In the children's project that follows, a tin can set in a pot of water is used as a makeshift double boiler. It is safe, as long as you boil the water slowly over a low flame (or at the low setting on an electric range) and turn off the heat as soon as the last bit of wax has melted. Crayons were used for coloring the wax. This is fine for children, but for the more acceptable candle-coloring techniques, see page 32.

Hand-dipped candles

A simple project for children demonstrates the age-old method of hand dipping candles. The Colonial process consisted of dipping a weighted wick repeatedly in a vat of molten wax. The basic process remains unchanged, but I would like to show you how to make two hand-dipped candles, using everyday objects and materials, and two large, molded candles as by-products of the dipping. Although this is a project easy enough for children, it is vital they have constant adult supervision for safety sake.

You will need two 32-ounce fruit-juice cans, some cooking oil (or a can

The candlemaking projects include these pastoral, wild-flower-and fern-decorated white candles. Instructions for making them are on **page 37**.

1: Tin cans and pans act as double boilers for melting wax. Overheated wax can be dangerous, so extinguish heat as soon as last bit of wax has melted.

2: Placing chunk of wax in can. If you must add more wax after you have melted some, be careful to place it gently, so molten wax does not spatter.

Hand dipping is probably the simplest way of making candles. These were dipped by a child, with adult supervision, and were made of alternating layers of red and purple wax. This will create interesting dripping patterns as the candles burn.

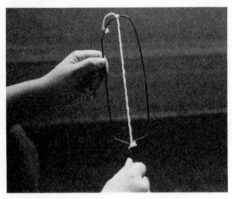

3: Bend wire hangers to this shape, and position the wick, as shown. Be sure it is stretched as taut as possible so wax will not bend as it builds up.

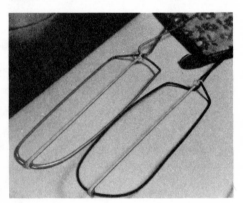

4: Two frames and wicks. Dip each one five times in one color and then five times in the other. Repeat procedure for half hour to make ¾-inch-thick candles.

of spray silicone or petroleum jelly), two large saucepans, three 16-ounce boxes of unrefined paraffin (sold in supermarkets), two wire coat hangers, about 4 feet of medium-size wick, two wax crayons in different but coordinating colors, a pair of scissors, and an ice pick (or piece of wire hanger). Follow these step-by-step instructions:

Clean the insides of the cans, and wipe with a thin coat of cooking oil.

Place the cans in 3 inches of water in the saucepans (photograph 1).

Cut the wax into chunks small enough to fit easily into the cans, and drop in enough wax to fill the cans (photograph 2).

Heat the water to boiling, and turn down the flame so the water will remain at a low boil. While the wax is melting, you can prepare the hangers.

Bend hangers to the shape shown, and tie on wicks (photographs 3 and 4).

When all the wax has melted, check the liquid-wax levels. They should be an inch below the can rims. If not, add more wax and wait for it to melt.

Remove the paper from the crayons, and drop them into the cans— one color in one can and the other in the other can (photograph 5). Wait for the crayons to melt, and then stir the wax gently to diffuse the color.

Turn off the flame, and wait about 15 minutes for the molten wax to cool.

Dip the wire frames and wicks into the wax (up to within an inch of the wick end), pull out, and hang to let the wax solidify. We hung the frames on a laundry rack, photograph 6. As the molten wax in the cans cools further, it will not be necessary to set the frames aside after each dipping. The wax will solidify quickly enough for you to simply hold the frame over the can for a few seconds, and then dip again (photograph 7). About half an hour of repeated dipping will complete the candles.

When the wax deposit has grown thick enough (about ¾ inches), hang the frames for the final drying period—about an hour, or until wax is firm.

With scissors or a knife, cut through the wicks at the top and the wax and wicks at the bottom, to free the candles from the frames.

You can turn the remaining liquid wax into candles by putting the cans in the refrigerator. When the wax has solidified, remove it from the cans by dipping them in hot water. To add wicks, push a heated ice pick or straight piece of wire hanger all the way down into the candles; insert the wicks (see photograph 14, page 32), and seal the openings with some melted wax.

Ten-year-old David Hunter begins dipping. He submerges frame up to an inch below wick end and withdraws it, all in one movement. Be sure stove is turned off.

5: Adding crayons—red to one can and purple to the other. You can make solid-color candles with one can, one crayon.

6: Wax-coated frames cooling on rack. Middle column is candle. Wax on frames can be scraped off with knife and reused.

7: In later stages of dipping process, hold frame over can for a few seconds until wax solidifies; then redip.

No need to be wary of
these beehives. They
are rolled wax, painted and cut to look
like whimsical versions of hives.

Beeswax honeycomb candles ¢ ⊠ ⚐ ⚒

Since ancient times, people have regarded bees as models of industry and purity. For that reason, and because it is so sweet smelling, beeswax has always been used for church and temple candles. To this day, church candles usually contain at least 50 percent beeswax. You can buy beeswax in blocks for making candles in molds, but this project shows you how to make very simple candles by rolling thin sheets of honeycombed wax.

In its natural honeycomb form, beeswax would be ideal for a rolled candle, but you probably would have to go straight to the source (a beehive) to find enough of it. In its place, I use commercially produced part-natural beeswax that has been embossed with a honeycomb pattern. It comes in 8-by-16-inch sheets in a variety of colors and is available at many hobby shops. If you have difficulty obtaining it, you can order it from A. I. Root, 1106 East Grand Street, Elizabeth, N.J. 07201.

To make a 5-inch candle 2 inches in diameter, you will need one 8-by-16-inch sheet of wax, a pair of scissors, and 7 inches of wicking.

Fold and tear the sheet of wax in half lengthwise (photograph 9). Place a piece of 7-inch wick at one short end. Fold half an inch of the edge over the wick. Crimp the wax so it holds the wick snugly. Roll the wax at a slight angle to make a conical shape at the wick end. Before the end of the sheet is reached, overlap it with the end of the other cut sheet. Finish rolling.

Beehives are the source of very fine wax for making candles. Natural beeswax burns evenly and is sweetly fragrant.

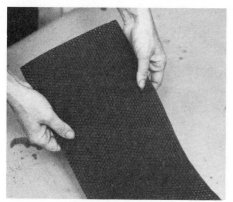

8: A sheet of 8-by-16-inch honeycomb wax. You can make a 9-inch candle by rolling it lengthwise or a 17-inch candle by rolling it across its width.

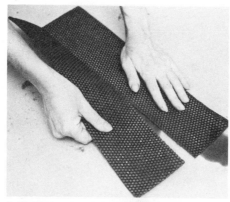

9: Fold the sheet of wax lengthwise, and tear along the fold. Both 4-by-16-inch pieces are needed to make a 2-inch-thick and 5-inch-high honeycomb candle.

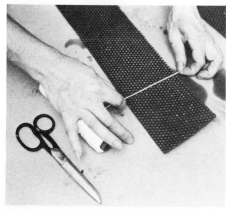

10: Use a piece of wick about 3 inches longer than the width of the wax sheet. You can cut off the excess wick at both ends after the candle is rolled.

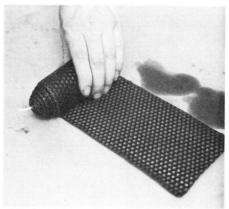

11: Roll the wax fairly tightly at a slight angle to create pointed end. The wax will bend easily and hold its cylindrical shape without any sealing.

Confectionary candles

One of the nicest characteristics of wax is that it can be a great impersonator. It especially lends itself to the imitation of such delicious edibles as ice-cream sundaes, sodas, and whipped cream. These confectionary delights made of wax may not be taste treats, but they are colorful and make lively decorative additions to a room. You can learn to concoct your own confectionary candles by following these instructions.

Although, in the children's project, I showed you how to color wax with crayons, they are not recommended for general use, because they often contain chemicals that impair the even burning of the wax. Ordinary food color and commercial dyes are also undesirable, since they color unevenly and often leave residue. It is best to color wax with products designed for that purpose. Candle color in both liquid and cake form is sold at hobby shops. Follow the directions included to use either correctly.

To make the ice-cream-sundae candle in the color photograph, far right, you will need enough wax in each color to half fill a medium-size sauce pan (see

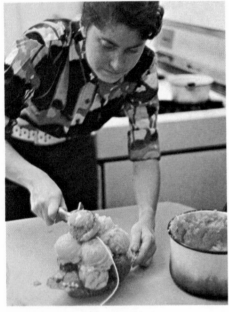

Miss Wharton enjoys making extravagant "ice-cream" concoctions like this. You can easily create similar ones.

12: Scoop the wax much as you would a helping of ice cream. If the wax begins to get hard, run some hot water over the scoop to heat it before using.

◀ Unless you are a very fast scooper, you may have to reheat the wax over a low flame, as you work, to maintain the right oatmeal consistency.

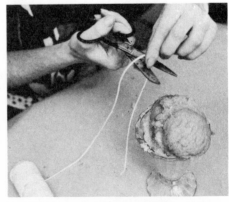

13: Making shaft for wick with piece of wire heated at one end. You can add wick and then put on cherry off-center, or place cherry first and pierce for wick.

14: Cutting some wick to apply to candle. If you have difficulty inserting it, dip it in some melted wax and then cool it in the refrigerator. This will stiffen it.

Confectionary candles capture the warmth and charm of turn-of-the-century ice-cream parlors. Bring a little of that whimsy to your home by making your own.

photograph 12); a double boiler; a saucepan for each color; a spoon; a suitable glass container; an ice-cream scoop; an eggbeater; a pastry tube (optional) for applying "whipped cream"; a cupful of red wax; a melon-ball scoop; an ice pick or length of wire hanger; and about a foot of wick.

In double boiler, heat wax for the "ice cream" for the inside of the glass. Pour the melted wax into the pan, let it cool. When it is the consistency of oatmeal, stir it and spoon it into the glass container.

Heat wax for the scoops. When it is of oatmeal consistency, pile two or three scoopfuls, in the same or varying colors, onto the wax in the glass.

As described on page 34, whip some white wax with an eggbeater, and pour it over the "ice cream." Or you can use a cake-decorating tube, as I did, to apply the whipped wax as shown in the photograph at right.

For the cherry, carve a melon scoopful of red wax, and set it at the top.

Make a hole for the wick with a heated ice pick or piece of hanger wire (photograph 13), and insert the wick. Apply a little liquid wax around the wick at the opening to seal it.

This elaborate sundae candle is not hard to make. Put whipped wax in pastry tube (available at supermarkets) to make fancy "whipped cream." Or pour on whipped wax.

33

Molded candles

A great variety of containers can be used as molds for making wax candles—milk and cream cartons, containers of plastic, plaster, glass, metal, or ceramic, and almost anything you can improvise. Some candles remain in their molds, such as the soda-pop candle on this page and the candle being made in figure A on the opposite page. Others, such as those made in the metal molds shown in photograph 17, are cast in the containers and are removed as soon as the wax has solidified.

It should be mentioned at this point that if you become really interested in candlemaking as a permanent hobby, you should invest in a dripless and seamless aluminum or stainless-steel pitcher. This is the most important implement in home candlemaking. Although you can improvise with an old coffeepot (see figure A), a pitcher is safer, and it is perfect for pouring or ladling molten wax into molds. Also, you may want to buy the type of crockery pot that has built-in, unexposed electric elements. This kind of pot is an ideal container for melting wax and is more convenient and even safer than a double boiler.

Soda-Pop Candle

This is another confectionary-type candle, but it is included here because it is cast in a mold, and the techniques used to make it are the same as those used for other molded candles.

15: Add stearic-acid granules if you are working with unrefined paraffin. Add 20 percent by weight, or follow directions on the container for correct amount.

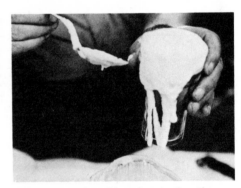

16: Spoon on the whipped wax after the colored wax in the glass has solidified. A little overflow will make the glass of soda look even more realistic.

Materials you will need are a 10-ounce soda glass, as shown; enough wax to fill the glass; coloring to suit your preference; a cupful of uncolored wax for whipping; an eggbeater or electric blender; an ice pick or short length of wire hanger; about a foot of wick; a short plastic drinking straw.

Melt the wax for filling the glass, and add coloring. Keep in mind that wax tends to lighten in color as it hardens. Test the color your liquid wax will be when it hardens by pouring a drop of it in a basin of cool water. The drop will immediately solidify and reveal its final color.

Allow 15 minutes for the wax to cool. When it has cooled pour it into the glass up to about an inch of the rim.

While this is hardening, prepare some whipped wax, which can be made as easily as whipped cream. Simply pour a cupful of uncolored melted wax into a bowl or pan. Wait until a skim forms on the surface, and then beat with an eggbeater until frothy. For whiteness, add, while whipping 2 or 3 tablespoons of stearic-acid. If you don't like the idea of beating by hand, you can use an electric mixer or blender, but they are a little more difficult to clean. Wax-covered utensils can be heated in a 150-degree oven and wiped clean.

Only the burning flame gives this creation away as something other than a cool and tempting glass of soda.

When the wax in the glass has solidified, spoon on the whipped wax (photograph 16), and insert the straw. Wait about two or three hours, to make sure the wax has set sufficiently; then make a hole for the wick with a heated ice pick or wire, and insert the wick.

Professional-Type Molds

Tin and stainless-steel molds, such as those shown in photograph 17, are what professional candlemakers use. They are available in a variety of sizes and shapes for making all kinds of candles and are sold at hobby shops or can be ordered from a number of manufacturers.

To make a candle in a professional-type mold, you will need—in addition to the blocks of wax, wick, melting and pouring containers, and color and scent additives (optional) mentioned in previous projects—a candy thermometer; a tin or steel mold the shape and size of your choice; a spray can of silicone candle-mold release; plastic putty or very sticky and heavy adhesive tape; a pencil or small piece of heavy wire. Anything that will seal the hole at the bottom of the mold without leaking, and is removable, can be used instead of the putty or tape. All of these, with the possible exception

17: These steel and tin molds are only a small sampling of the many shapes and sizes available. Never use molds made of copper. They can stain the wax.

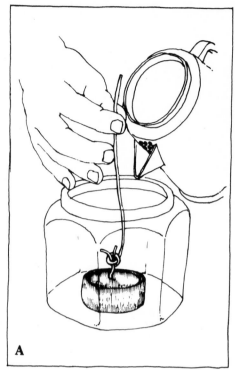

A

Figure A: Glass jars or bowls can be used as molds and containers for candles. The technique, with this kind of container, is to tie some wick onto the wick of a small votive candle. Insert this candle, with its extended wick, into container. Hold wick upright, or secure it as shown in photograph 20 on page 36. Pour wax; allow to set. Add more wax, as needed, according to directions for metal-molded candle. Clip off excess wick. Alternate method is to follow this procedure, but to use a wick fastener (photograph 21, page 36) instead of a votive candle.

of the candy thermometer, are available at craft or hobby shops. Some hobby shops may have the thermometers, but if not, they can be purchased at any store that sells housewares or baking utensils. Follow these step-by-step instructions to make a candle in any standard mold:

Fill the mold to the brim with water (hold your finger over the wick hole at the bottom), and empty it into the heating container. This will give you an indication of the level of melted wax you will need to fill the mold. Be sure to dry both container and mold before adding wax.

Heat the wax, and prepare the mold while you wait for the wax to melt.

Spray the inside of the mold with the silicone mold release. This will ensure easy removal of the candle, once it has set.

Thread the wicking through the hole in the bottom of the mold (photograph 18, page 36), and extend it well beyond the mouth of the mold at the other end. Knot it at the base end so it cannot slip through the hole.

To make candle at right, add various-color wax cubes to mold; then pour melted wax. For candle at left, use gelatin mold.

35

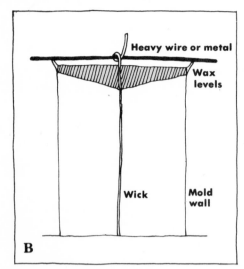

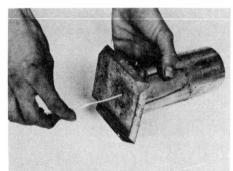

Figure B: This diagram shows a side view of a mold, with wax, wick, and wire in place. The shaded area represents the contraction of the wax as it cools. It also represents the new liquid wax that must be added after each cooling period, until the center of the candle is solid and the top is relatively flat.

18: Wick for molded candle is threaded through hole in bottom of mold (see instructions on page 35). Before knotting wick, be sure it extends through mold and about 6 inches beyond mouth, to provide enough to tie around wire.

19: Plastic putty is ideal for sealing the hole and the knotted wick. It holds tightly, but can be removed easily when wax has set. Floral clay or heavy and very sticky adhesive tape will work almost as well as the plastic putty.

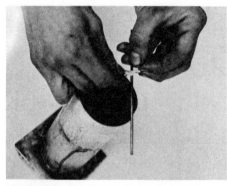

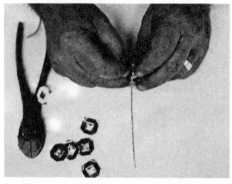

20: Use heavy wire, as shown, a pencil, or a wood stick to hold the wick upright while you pour the melted wax. Rest the wire on the mold; center it, and tie the wick tightly to the wire.

21: These wick fasteners can be bought at a hobby shop. Or you can remove them from burned-down votive candles. Fasten one to a wick, to secure the wick at bottom of any mold without a wick hole.

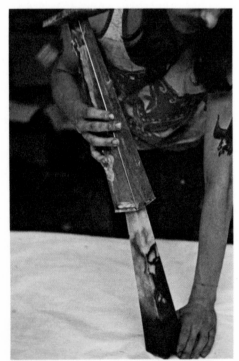

22: Removing a candle from its mold. Wait at least eight hours for wax molecules to set before attempting this final step.

Apply whatever sealer you choose to the hole and wick (photograph 19).

Pull the wick taut; wrap it around a pencil or piece of heavy wire at the mold opening, and tie it (photograph 20). Rest the wire or pencil on the mold, and center the wick as shown in figure B. The mold is now ready.

Set the thermometer in the pouring container (steel pitcher or coffeepot); pour in the melted wax, and let it cool to the ideal pouring temperature (190 to 195 degrees Fahrenheit).

Pour a little wax to cover the bottom of the mold, and let it set for five minutes. This will seal off the wick opening and lessen the chances of any leaks due to the pressure of the liquid wax.

Fill the rest of the mold to about half an inch of the rim. Pour down the center to avoid stripping the silicone coating on the mold walls. When the wax has solidified (about an hour), make an opening down the center with a spoon handle. There will already be a center cavity because of the contraction of the wax as it solidified. Refill this cavity with wax, and let cool. Repeat this procedure once or twice more until a cavity does not reappear. Let the wax set for at least eight hours.

Roll the mold in your hand, pressing lightly, and upend it. The candle should slide out easily (photograph 22). If it does not, run some warm water over the outside of the mold, and try again.

When you have removed the candle from its mold, cut off the excess wick at both ends. What was at the top of the mold will be the bottom of your candle, and vice versa. For a smooth, high-gloss finish, rub the candle a little with an old nylon stocking.

Wild-flower candles

There are many ways to decorate plain candles that you have made or have purchased. They can be carved, painted, stenciled, decoupaged, or appliqued with small pieces of cast or carved wax.

Although it is easy to get carried away, it is wise to exercise restraint; an unadorned candle is attractive in itself, and any applied decoration should not detract from its intrinsic beauty.

One of the nicest ways to decorate candles is to use natural materials, such as dried wild flowers, weeds, or ferns, as shown in the color photograph, right. Buttercups, violets, hay, and other small-scale, easily dried flowers or grasses are suitable. Gather these from your garden or house plants (photograph 23), and dry them in one of the commercially prepared products designed for this purpose, such as silica gel (available at garden centers).

To make candles like those shown in the color photograph, you will need—in addition to the candles, wild flowers, and drying material mentioned above—some pieces of brown wrapping paper, an iron, a small amount of paraffin or household wax that will have no color added to it, a small saucepan, a glass container large enough to contain wax to be melted, and a large artist's brush (see photograph 24). Follow these simple step-by-step instructions to decorate a candle with dried flowers:

Place the dried flowers or ferns you have selected between two pieces of brown wrapping paper, and press, using a dry iron set at low heat. Iron on an ironing board, or use a hard surface, such as stiff cardboard.

Place glass container into saucepan containing about ½-inch of water. Add wax to glass container and bring water to boil. Melt wax until liquid and keep liquid throughout process.

Position flower on candle and quickly paint hot wax over entire flower. A thin coat is sufficient, but repeat the procedure, if necessary, until the flowers are completely covered and firmly sealed to the candle.

These candles are not suited to being burned all the way down. However, if they are, there is no danger of the dried flowers catching fire. They will only become hot and curl up.

Arlene Hayden, a graduate of the Philadelphia College of Art, is an editorial designer for Ladies' Home Journal *and a free-lance designer for* American Home Crafts *magazine. She makes candles as a hobby and, while spending time on her parents' farm, got the idea of decorating candles with dried flowers.*

23: If you are an apartment dweller, your potted plants can be a good source of material to dry and apply to plain candles. This Boston fern will not suffer from giving up a few fronds.

24. This candle has had liquid wax brushed on it after dried fern fronds were positioned in place. Here, Miss Hayden gives final touches to seal them to the candle.

Dried specimens of growing things make tasteful, appealing candle decorations.

37

CANOEING
Outdoor Family Challenge

Stuart James was outdoors editor for Popular Mechanics *for six years, executive editor of* True *for two years, and is now editor of* Rudder. *He grew up in the outdoors, running a trapline along Neshaminy Creek in southeast Pennsylvania at eight, fishing and hunting at every available moment. He first paddled a canoe at seven. Since then, he figures he has paddled over 1500 miles. He considers work boats the most interesting craft and the canoe the best and most versatile of work boats. His ten-year-old son, Morgan, who had never been in a canoe before, assisted him in the demonstration here.*

Canoeing is a natural activity. Put anyone in a canoe for the first time with a paddle in his hands and he will paddle spontaneously and correctly the first time he dips the paddle into the water. His motions will be a bit clumsy at first—he will dig the paddle in, splash, lean heavily into the stroke, and tilt the canoe to one side. But within an hour he will have adjusted himself to paddling, and by the end of a day the average person—man, woman, even a child—will find he can paddle well. After a few canoe trips, he can be quite expert.

I believe this is one reason why the canoe design has remained virtually unchanged since this Indiancraft was discovered by French explorers who came to North America early in the seventeenth century. Samuel de Champlain never ceased to marvel at the speed and maneuverability of the birch-bark canoe, and he adopted it immediately for his push into the interior. A canoe was, and is, the perfect craft for stream, river, and lake. Construction materials have changed, but the design is the same—there is simply no reason to alter it.

The most popular canoe today is made of aluminum, with fiberglass running a close second. You can still buy canvas-covered wooden canoes, and although they are heavy and expensive and require considerable maintenance care, they have their place in lake running. For river running and general touring, aluminum and fiberglass canoes are superior. They are lighter, maintenance-free, and inexpensive. If a rock tears a hole in either type

The canoe is the only watercraft native to North America. The canoe design we know today was fully developed when the first European explorers arrived on this continent. It is singularly well adapted to inland waters, and although ideally it is managed by two paddlers, it can be handled easily by one ten-year-old paddling from the stern.

of craft, it is easily repaired. (See Canoeing Craftnotes on pages 48 and 49.) If you plan to canoe on a large lake, the canvas-covered wood type is best. It has a deeper keel, higher gunwales, a high, wide bow for taking large waves, and cork sponsons (floats) along the gunwales to improve stability.

Getting to Know the Craft

Before you take out a canoe, spend a couple of hours with an aluminum or fiberglass model getting to know the craft and its responses.

Safely strapped into life jackets, in shallow, calm water, practice exchanging seats with your partner, rising simultaneously, moving forward and aft in a low crouch, balancing each other's weight and motion as you advance. A canoe is a light, buoyant craft, and difficult to balance in if you stand too tall or move quickly and thoughtlessly. However, its buoyancy makes it hard to capsize and impossible to sink as long as it is intact.

Handling a capsize situation is another drill a beginner should practice in shallow water, in part to learn just how hard it is to overturn that seemingly unstable craft, and in part to gain confidence in his ability to handle a capsize should it occur. To capsize the canoe, lean heavily to one side until it tips over. It rarely will completely overturn. More often, paddlers spill into the water and the canoe fills with water but stays upright. Air chambers under the fore and aft decks will keep the water-filled canoe afloat and will support your weight as well. To get underway again, one paddler holds the canoe steady while the other bails with bailer, tin can, hat or hands. Partially bailed, the canoe is guided to shore and emptied. If the canoe does turn upside down, dive and come inside it. You will find it filled with air. Holding to the seats inside, paddle the canoe to shore.

1: Even when filled with water, the capsized canoe is unsinkable and an excellent life raft. It can be paddled even when it is partially submerged.

In safety drill, canoe is capsized in shallow water, above; paddled to shore although filled with water, below.

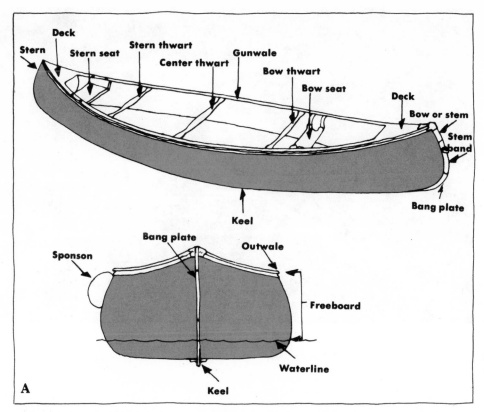

Figure A: This diagram shows the basic canoe. Some of the elements are modified for special work. A lake canoe handles better with a deeper keel; for long passages in open water, it is advisable to have a canoe with high, curving bow and stern and high gunwales. For constant white-water paddling, a wide, flat keel offers protection from rocks. The sponson, a shaped half-round of cork running the length of the canoe just below the gunwales, is optional, but it keeps the craft from capsizing.

How to Paddle a Canoe

There are two paddling positions in a canoe—bow (front) and stern (back). The stern paddler controls the canoe's direction, sets the pace, and calls instructions to the bow paddler. The more experienced canoeist generally takes the stern seat, the novice or smaller canoeist, the bow.

The bow paddler in a cruising canoe uses the basic power stroke most of the time. This is really doing what comes naturally. Paddling on the right side, you hold the grip of the paddle loosely in the palm of the left hand and grasp the shaft with the right hand. You dip the paddle blade into the water ahead of you, pull it back with the right arm, lift the blade clear of the water, move it forward, and repeat the maneuver. That's all there is to it. You change hands for the left-side power stroke.

The most important part of paddling is to feel comfortable and set a pace that agrees with you. Don't lunge into the strokes or do all your vigorous paddling in the first five minutes. Dip the paddle, stay upright and pull back, keeping the paddle straight and close to the side of the canoe.

Sitting in the rear, the stern paddler adjusts his stroke and pace to the bowman. He uses a variety of strokes, but all are so suited to the control of the craft that he would do them without knowing their names. For straight cruising, he uses the power stroke in unison with the bow paddler, but on the opposite side. If he is getting off course, he applies the J stroke or the steering stroke. The J stroke is merely a forward carry through after the power stroke; this pulls the bow to right or left. The steering stroke (you will hear several names for all these strokes) is simply keeping the blade of the paddle slightly angled during the stroke and holding it for a few seconds at the end of the stroke, like a rudder; this also guides the bow to right or left.

For making an abrupt turn, the stern paddler digs the paddle in at the end of a stroke and pushes down and forward, while the bow paddler executes a wide, sweeping arc that sends the bow around. Again, these are such normal movements that a novice canoeist would do them almost automatically.

A common problem with many novices is digging in the paddle just before

2: The bow stroke is a simple movement of dipping the paddle blade toward the bow and pulling straight back without touching the canoe. The body is kept as vertical as possible, with the arms performing most of the work.

3: The J stroke, performed at stern, is particularly useful for adjusting direction when strong bowman overpowers stern paddler in basic cruising stroke. Stern man pulls paddle through stroke, sculls (strokes at an angle) to the right, then pushes forward and holds before the next stroke.

4: The bow rudder stroke is a simple maneuver for pulling the bow to right or left. In the execution, the paddler just reverses the position of the pulling hand on the shank of the paddle to push, dips the blade forward of the bow position, and holds against the canoe's momentum. It is most effective in fast water when the bowman sees a submerged obstacle.

▲ 5: A quarter sweep turns canoe sharply without loss of speed. Paddles—on right, as above, or on left, opposite—are moved in unison through a wide, shallow arc.

6: The stern rudder stroke is strictly a steering maneuver. At the end of a normal cruising stroke, the paddle is held on a diagonal while bow paddler goes through his next stroke. In fast water, this directs the canoe without paddling.

7: The jam stroke stops the canoe dead in the water and brings the bow to right or left. The paddle blade is placed fully into the water at the rear of a stroke, then pushed forward with force.

he starts a stroke and splashing forward. He also pulls in on the follow-through at the end of a stroke and splashes water into the canoe. You can eliminate this by counting off a rhythm: "Stroke ...one, two ... dip, stroke," and so on. It makes you think about the paddle's position. Another problem with a novice is that he feels he must put body into the strokes. He leans on the paddle as he makes a stroke, rolls upright on the return, and leans into the next stroke. From the bow seat he can't see that this motion sets up such a roll that the center gunwale goes under and the canoe takes the water. Sit upright, relaxed, and let arms and shoulders do the work.

These strokes are all you need to know for canoeing in average water on rivers and lakes.

Selecting a Paddle

The most important thing in selecting a paddle is to get the proper fit. For the stern man, the paddle should reach from floor to forehead; for the bowman, from floor to chin. Quality is not essential for the novice, but make sure you have a spare paddle for each paddler. Ash and maple are the best woods and the quality of the wood and the craftsmanship are important. When you reach the stage where you call a paddle a blade, you are ready to shop for a good one.

10: The bow sweep, which is also called the quarter sweep, is used to swing the bow sharply. When it is used in conjunction with a strong power stroke at the stern, the canoe both turns and gains speed. If the stern man applies the steering stroke or a jam stroke, the turn is tight and abrupt.

Portaging the Canoe

An 18-foot canoe weighs about 120 pounds. Since the weight is well distributed, it is not difficult to carry (portage) for short distances. When you haul this weight uphill on rough ground, through brush, and over boulders, however, a carry of only a quarter mile can be tiring.

Unless exceptionally strong and used to carrying a canoe, the two-man carry is recommended. With the canoe right side up and one man at each end and on opposite sides, each takes a handhold under the deck and lifts. A variation is the two-man shoulder carry. Some shoulder padding helps—a blanket or a rolled-up jacket will do. The canoe is turned upside down; the stern is lifted and placed on the shoulder of one man. The bowman (opposite side) then lifts it to his shoulder. This carry is particularly good in brush as it raises the canoe above the tops of most bushes you are likely to encounter.

If you are four men travelling with two canoes, you will save energy by making two trips and putting four men on each canoe. An important point about portaging: Allow plenty of time, and make the loads as light as possible. You may read about carrying a gear-packed canoe, but don't do it. You are out for a good time, and if you arrive at the campsite exhausted after a

8: The in-draw stroke is used most often in white water where abrupt changes of direction are necessary. The paddler reaches out with the blade parallel to the canoe, plunges it into the water, and pulls it toward the canoe with as much speed and force as he can muster.

11: A stroke particularly adapted to single-handed paddling is the stern sweep. It swings the bow in a sharp turn without loss of speed or a break in paddling rhythm. This is the same as the quarter sweep, but is a more effective stroke with the bow out of the water.

9: With only one paddler, every power stroke swings the bow. So it is necessary to paddle on alternate sides or hold the blade as a rudder after each stroke. If the paddle is held on a diagonal, it keeps the canoe in a straight line and eliminates compensating strokes.

12: Directly opposite of the in-draw, the pushover is also a fast-water stroke. The blade goes into the water parallel to the canoe and is pushed out with speed and force. Both strokes are especially useful at the bow.

43

14: Paddles have been lashed between the thwarts to form a yoke for the one-man carry. If the shoulders are padded, a canoe can be easily carried this way for surprisingly long distances.

15: The two-man shoulder carry is relatively easy, even with a ten-year-old at one end, although frequent rests are recommended during long portages. Carriers are on opposite sides, for balance.

16: Two-man carry for a short portage or to place the canoe in the water has one man on each side, grasping the bow and stern decks. Not recommended for narrow paths or long distances.

17: Lifting the canoe for a one-man carry is made easier by raising one end and resting it on the branch of a tree. The carrier then crouches into the yoke and lifts the canoe away from the tree.

13: Initial step in the one-man carry is lifting the canoe onto the thighs. Then the thwarts are grasped, and in one swinging motion, the craft is lifted overhead and settled on the shoulders, where it is adjusted for balance.

full day of paddling and carrying, totally exhausted, you are defeating your purpose.

The one-man carry for any distance is grueling, but it can be done, and in time (believe it or not) you can almost get used to it. You fashion a yoke by lashing two paddles on the thwarts (photograph 14). I like the yoke to be slightly V-shape, with the blades of the paddles forward. This allows me to move into the yoke and get the canoe in a comfortable position on my shoulders. And with my hands on the paddle blades, I have a controlling leverage for the weight. The prescribed method of getting the canoe onto the shoulders is to lift one side so the bottom is resting against the knees, grasp the thwarts, and lift the canoe onto the thighs. You are now stooping. Reach across and grasp the thwarts on the far side, and roll the canoe onto your shoulder. Grasp both gunwales, and with one movement, lift with both arms at the same time, and duck your head under the canoe. Lower the yoke onto your shoulders, get comfortable, and you are ready to go. If a tree is available, and one ususally is, I just drag the canoe to the base of its trunk and lift the bow end until it can be propped against the lowest limb. I step under the canoe, get comfortable in the yoke, and lift. Then I back away from the tree and am on my way.

The techniques of portaging vary with the terrain and with the distance of the carry. The objective is to move the canoe and supplies overland around an obstacle—and you must adapt your method of accomplishing the task to the nature of the obstacle confronting you.

Lining a canoe is not really a portage, but you will think about it when you first encounter rapids you don't want to run and you don't feel like making a carry, so I will mention it here. Lining is merely tying long lines to the fore and aft thwarts and letting the canoe float down through the rapids while you and your partner, holding the lines on opposite sides of the stream, control its descent. This sounds easy, but it can be tricky if the water is swift. The only way to learn it is to try it. Tracking a canoe is the same maneuver, except that the canoe is pulled upstream through rapids.

White-Water Canoeing

The ultimate thrill for the canoeist is running white water. This is when his sport moves into the category of soaring or rock climbing or scuba diving and skill is thoroughly tested. There is always the tingling feeling of apprehension as you approach the drop-off for the first run of the day, holding back and standing to survey the rapids and decide on a course. This changes to exhilaration as the canoe picks up speed and plunges into what appears to be a maelstrom. From then on, you are too busy to think much about emotions, but the remembrance of the run is a blend of high excitement, shouting, rushing water, the soul-wrenching crunch when the canoe slammed

Poised before the first drop into a run of white water on Connecticut's Housatonic River, father and son experience the elation and camaraderie that are part of this exciting activity.

into submerged rock, the springboard resilience of the hull as it bounded off unscathed, laughter, controlled panic, a feeling of unfettered joy.

The dangers of white water are real and ever present, but they can be reduced to nearly zero with care and planning. The best way the novice can be introduced to white water is for him to compete in a downriver race for open canoes sponsored by a recognized canoe club. Since the course is planned for open canoes, it will be exciting, but not too dangerous. There will be plenty of canoeists on the river, so you will have company and assistance if needed—and you can follow others and imitate them. If sections of the rapids are difficult, you can be certain the shore will be lined with spectators looking for thrills, and should you capsize and get into trouble, there will be many hands to help you. Hundreds of races are held each spring, when the water is good, high and fast, all over the country.

Special equipment is essential in white water. You should wear a plastic helmet to protect your head, a good life jacket, and tile-setter's kneepads. Footwear is also important, because you will be in and out of the canoe a great deal, hauling it over shallows or freeing it from a cleft in rocks, and the footing will be slippery and uneven. A pair of sturdy, ankle-high work shoes will give you good protection from stone bruises and twisted ankles, and you will be glad to have something solid on your feet when one foot slips between two rocks and you are wrestling with a wild canoe.

Keeping a low profile is vitally important in white water. Both paddlers kneel on the bottom of the canoe. The bowman kneels behind the forward thwart; this frees him from entanglement with the bow seat, raises the bow slightly, and gives him more mobility. The stern man kneels just forward of the stern seat. In these positions both men have their center of gravity below the gunwales, have greater stroking power, and, in the event of trouble, can crouch down into the canoe for more stability. It is always startling to find yourself suddenly going through the rapids stern first; but in most cases when a canoe is clearly out of control, if the paddlers concentrate on the lowest possible profile and on balance, the canoe will go through the rapids unaided or will at least come to rest in a stable enough position so they can regain control and proceed.

All the advanced paddling strokes come into play when a pair of experts are weaving in and around the rocks in a stretch of fast water. The bowman will be using the jam stroke, the bow rudder, the draw stroke, the sweep stroke. The stern man will be backwatering, jamming, drawing in, and pushing out. When two men work well together, there is a lightning-fast, coordinated effort, punctuated by shouts; the paddles flash in and out of the water, flicking to right or left; the canoe, responding, dodges this way and that.

18: Safety equipment is required for white-water canoeing. A life jacket is a necessity; a lightweight plastic helmet protects the head from rocks, and tile-setter's kneepads protect the knees from painful abrasions.

19: For a well-balanced canoe in a run of white water, paddlers kneel aft of the stern and bow thwarts. With the weight slightly aft, the bow rises a little.

The various strokes can be practiced in any kind of water, but it is in white water where they will be perfected; where the canoeist can watch the canoe react to his strokes; where the bow must be hooked to the right to avoid a sharp rock and the fast, hard draw stroke does the trick; where the canoe goes through a chute and is brought to a sudden stop by jam strokes at bow and stern and then is quickly pivoted to the right by fast back-paddling at the stern and a hard quarter sweep at the bow.

Capsizing is the major danger in white water. Properly equipped with helmet and life vest, the canoeist should not suffer more than bruises and wounded dignity. Unless you are in a cataract (and no advice is going to help anyone foolish enough to make a clearly suicidal attempt), a dunking in the rapids is usually just an exhilarating swim. Get away from the canoe if you can, relax, and go along with the water. After all, if you capsize, you are no longer canoeing, you are swimming through the rapids. Relax and enjoy yourself as much as you can. Your life vest will keep you up and your helmet will save your head from knocks. Work your way to shore and try again.

I once had a bad experience with a free stern line in a canoe capsize. I was under the canoe with my back jammed against a rock, and the force of the cascading water was slamming the canoe against me. But the major problem was that my feet and legs had become entwined in the long stern line that had been bunched under the stern deck behind the seat, and I couldn't get away from the canoe. I managed to force my head above water and shouted to my partner for help. He held me out of the water while I freed my feet and legs. Since then, I have never had a free line in my canoe. The lines, bow and stern, are neatly coiled around one side of the seat and tied off, that is one hazard I do not have to contend with.

It is never wise for a pair of novices in a single canoe to attempt white water where they are alone. Stay with a group. You will meet many people with similar interests and you will find safety in numbers.

Canoe Camping

Canoe camping, once you get out of the canoe, is like any other camping, with two exceptions: In canoe camping, the sleeping bags are usually wet, and at least a third of your time is spent with a canoe on your back.

There are a few things the canoe camper should add to his regular camping equipment. Make sure you have sturdy, rubberized, waterproof bags to hold clothing, sleeping bags, cameras, etc. You will need extra paddles, a supply of drinking water, waterproof matches, and extra flashlight batteries. Sterno canned heat is easy to carry and lights whether wet or dry, so it comes in handy. Always take along a canoe-repair kit. If you are lucky, you won't have to use it, but it is good to know it is available.

Listed below is equipment suggested for a canoe camping trip for two.

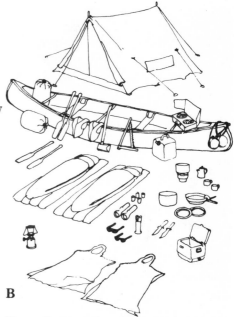

B

Figure B: Everything you need for comfortable canoe camping: Lightweight nylon mountain tent, lightweight (summer) sleeping bags with waterproof carrying bags, air mattresses, life jackets, extra paddles, hiker's ax, folding saw, plastic water jug (foldable), two-burner gas stove, canteens, cooking utensils (basket type), mess kits, flashlights, gasoline lantern, ponchos. For wilderness travel, it would be wise to include maps, compass, repair kits, first-aid materials, and a kit of emergency flares.

Canoe	2 ponchos
4 paddles	Waterproof bags
2 life jackets	2 sleeping bags
Nylon tent	1 ¾ woodsman's ax
2 air mattresses	Folding saw
2 mess kits	2 flashlights; extra batteries
Coleman stove or Sterno	Insect repellent
Water can, 2 to 3 gallons	2 canteens
2 knives	Sunglasses
Cook set	Cooler (optional)

My feeling is that if camping equipment cannot be carried in a pack, I don't want it. The cooler and Coleman stove would not be part of my gear. I also prefer a lean-to to a tent. Some campers like to take a radio along, but for myself I prefer the raucous wilderness.

CANOEING CRAFTNOTES: FIBERGLASS REPAIR

1: First step in fiberglass repair is to cut out the area around the hole or fracture until all edges are smooth, solid fiberglass—even if this means slightly enlarging the hole. Major difficulty is cutting the hole in the canoe, but get in there with saber saw or jigsaw with a fine-tooth blade, and make the cut.

2: With sanding disk on an electric hand drill and coarse sandpaper (about 80-grit), sand the surface around the hole—on the inside of the hull—until it is sufficiently roughened to facilitate a good bond. The sanded area should extend at least 2 inches beyond circumference of the hole you have cut.

3: Next step is to cover hole from outside. Shape piece of aluminum or heavy cardboard to hull contour; cover with plastic wrap; place over hole, with plastic facing in, and secure it in place with masking tape.

4: Cut patches of fiberglass cloth and mat about 2 inches bigger than hole. Mix enough resin and catalyst (about 10 to 1) to wet both. Lay patches on plastic and saturate thoroughly with resin. Place mat over hole and cover with cloth. Put plastic wrap over area, and smooth out air bubbles with a putty knife; work out from center.

5: In one to two hours, remove cardboard from outside, and roughen surface around hole, feathering toward the inside. Mask area around the hole with heavy paper and tape to protect the finish. Cut a mat patch about 1 inch larger than the hole and several cloth patches about 2 to 3 inches larger. Mix a new batch of resin and catalyst.

6: Brush resin into hole, and place mat patch over the hole. Mat will be stiff enough to maintain original contour. Saturate mat with dabbed-on resin. Apply a cloth patch, and saturate with dabbed-on resin. Keep adding cloth and resin until the layers are built up slightly above the hull's surface.

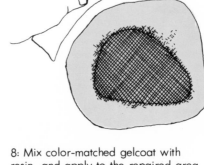

7: Smooth the patch, working all bubbles out to the edges, and let it cure about 20 minutes. When partially cured or rubbery to the touch, cut and strip off all excess cloth and mat on the outside edges of the feathering. Let the patch cure overnight (or about 12 hours), and then sand area until it is smooth and blends well with the undamaged area.

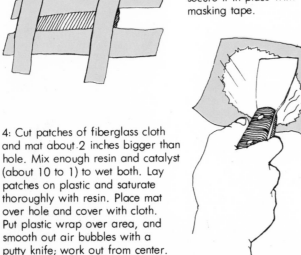

8: Mix color-matched gelcoat with resin, and apply to the repaired area, smoothing it with your hand or a squeegee. Cover the gelcoat with plastic wrap, and smooth again. Let the gelcoat cure completely; then rough-sand with wet, medium-coarse (about 220-grit) sandpaper. When the area is smooth to the touch, finish sanding with fine (about 600-grit) paper and buff thoroughly with rubbing compound until area matches original finish.

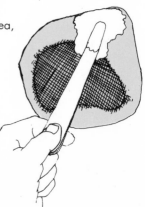

CANOEING CRAFTNOTES: ALUMINUM REPAIR

1: Pound out damaged area to proper contour. If a crack is apparent, drill at each end with No. 30 drill to stop crack from running farther. Cut an aluminum patch larger than damaged area; form it to the curve of the area; draw a pencil line around it.

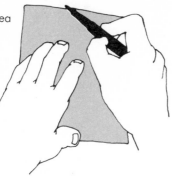

2: Remove the aluminum patch, and drill a hole in each corner. Size of the drill is determined by size of the pop rivets you will use. The size of the rivets is determined by the size of the hole you are patching. Fewer large rivets means drilling fewer holes. The corner holes should be about ½ inch in from the edges of the patch. With pencil and rule draw lines in the patch connecting the holes.

3: Guided by the penciled outline, place the patch back against the hull, covering the damaged area, and drill through the hull through one of the corner holes. Fasten the patch at this corner with a small bolt and nut to hold it in place. Then proceed to drill through the hull through the other three corner holes of the patch.

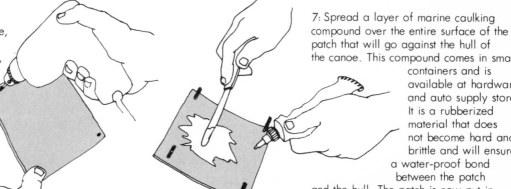

4: When the holes have been drilled in the hull through all four corners of the patch, it is secured to the hull by a bolt and nut in each corner. If you are using a No. 30 drill, the temporary fastenings should be ⅛-inch bolts with matching nuts. These locate plate so that the remaining holes can be drilled.

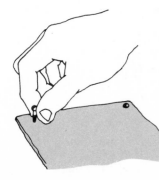

5: A pattern of holes with their centers an inch apart, go around the entire patch, drilling through the patch and the hull using the pencil lines on the patch as your guide. If it is an unusually large patch, drill a second row of holes an inch inside the first row, but staggered between the holes in the outer row. When all the holes have been drilled, the corner fastenings are removed and the patch is taken off the hull.

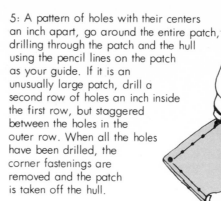

6: With a sharp, small-tooth file, remove the burrs from the holes on both sides of the patch and the inside and outside of the canoe. You can also hone down edges of the patch to make a better surface when the job is completed.

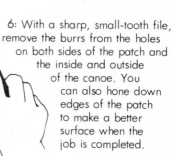

7: Spread a layer of marine caulking compound over the entire surface of the patch that will go against the hull of the canoe. This compound comes in small containers and is available at hardware and auto supply stores. It is a rubberized material that does not become hard and brittle and will ensure a water-proof bond between the patch and the hull. The patch is now put in place and fastened again at each corner with the temporary nut-and-bolt fasteners.

8: With a pop-rivet gun and closed-end pop rivets for a water-tight fit, patch is riveted progressively around the exterior. The temporary fastenings are removed, and those holes are riveted. The job is complete except for cleaning, smoothing, painting.

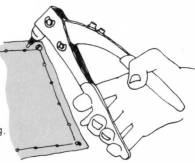

Natural Dairy Products

Freda Baron Friedman is the editor of the Journal of Practical Nursing and has written and edited many articles about nutrition. An inveterate cheese eater, she takes special pleasure in making her own.

For thousands of years, people the world over have been making milk products that bear little or no resemblance to milk. Many of these are the result of fermentation. Others, such as butter and mayonnaise, depend on churning or beating to convert them from cream (as in butter) and egg yolks (as in mayonnaise) to their final state.

Making these foods at home, in much the way the Colonists did, is in itself interesting, and they are nutritionally valuable additions to the diet, as they are rich in vitamins and minerals. Since these homemade products do not contain any preservatives, natural-food purists consider them especially healthful. In any case, the flavors are fresh and excellent.

Basic equipment you will need to make cheeses and dairy products is found in most kitchens. You will need a cooking thermometer with calibrations from 90 to 120F and a few yards of cheesecloth which is sold in packages by supermarkets and hardware stores. If you go in for the making of hard cheese then you will have to improvise, or make a cheese press. A double-boiler, and wooden spoons, are also useful, but you can also use metal spoons and place a small pot set in a larger one to simulate a double boiler. Recipes begin below.

Yogurts and sour cream

Making yogurt is a good way to start to learn cheesemaking. Though yogurt is not a cheese, the fermentation process responsible for yogurt is similar to the first step in making many soft cheeses. With the fermentation process, you can make all sorts of dairy products, from cottage cheese to sour cream. The recipe for Basic Yogurt is given on page 52.

Yogurt depends on the growth of bacteria to form lactic acid. When milk is inoculated with one or more types of the yogurt bacteria, they begin to grow, forming lactic acid and killing any harmful bacteria that may have infected the milk. The milk used differs from area to area, as do the bacteria. In the United States, cow's milk is used; in Armenia, buffalo's or goat's milk; in Lapland, reindeer's or mare's milk. Flavor and consistency vary with the type of milk and the bacteria.

A Historic Food

Yogurt has been the diet of peasants and the delicacy of kings for more than four thousand years. Throughout history there have been rituals and rules about yogurt. In some countries, cultures of bacteria were passed down from generation to generation, as part of a girl's dowry. Legend tells that Genghis Khan fed his vast army on yogurt to give the men strength during their long marches through the Orient and Persia. Other legends have linked yogurt consumption with long life, virility, the restoration of thinning hair, and the treatment of ulcers and other stomach ailments. Persian women were reported to preserve the freshness of their skin by eating yogurt and using it as a facial cream. Even today, some people believe yogurt preserves the complexion and bleaches away freckles.

Fresh, homemade sweet butter, with jam and bread or crackers, isn't a treat confined to farmers; anyone can make the dairy products pictured here. From left to right, front row, sweet butter and paraffin-coated, homemade hard cheese; back row, cream cheese made from yogurt, sour cream and cottage cheese.

1: An electric heating pad acts as an improvised yogurtmaker. Set at low heat, the pad has yogurt containers nestled into it and secured by the electric cord. To develop yogurt culture requires low, steady warmth. Any improvisation that can supply this warmth will do.

Rich in Nutrients

The rationale for these beliefs can be explained by yogurt's high protein, calcium, and lactic-acid content, which are beneficial to the skin. While yogurt's beneficial values do remain heartily controversial, it nevertheless is a very popular food. According to recent Department of Agriculture figures, Americans annually consume 25 million dollars' worth of yogurt.

Basic Yogurt is easy to make and is the basis for the dessert, salad dressing, soup, and cream cheese for which recipes are given on the opposite page. The bacteria are sensitive to temperature changes and the food they feed on. For best results, use fresh milk and fresh commercial yogurt as a starter. Aged yogurt used as a starter is less dependable.

Incubating Yogurt

First, plan how to keep the milk mixture warm enough for the culture to develop—between 105 and 112F—for 3 to 5 hours. Yogurtmaking appliances with temperature controls can be used, but you don't need one. An incubator can be easily improvised. You can nestle the yogurt jar in an electric heating pad, at the lowest setting, for 3 hours. Or place yogurt in a casserole; cover, and set in a pan of warm water on a radiator or in the oven at the lowest temperature for 3 to 5 hours. Or use a Balkan method: Pour warm yogurt mixture into a casserole; cover; wrap with a blanket, and leave in a warm room overnight. By morning the yogurt will be thick and ready for chilling.

Basic Yogurt

1 quart fresh milk	1 tablespoon plain, unflavored
2 tablespoons powdered milk	commercial yogurt

Combine fresh milk and powdered milk in a heavy, stainless-steel or enamel pot. Over low heat and stirring constantly, bring slowly to boiling point. Pour mixture into a bowl to cool to about 80 to 85F. Blend ½ cup of the warm milk with the yogurt until mixture is smooth. Then add this mixture to the bowl of remaining warm milk. Pour into a canning or freezer jar; cover, and keep warm, using one of the incubating methods described above. Incubate 3 to 5 hours—or overnight if you use blanket insulation. When the mixture is the consistency of thick cream, refrigerate it to chill before serving.

Makes four 8-ounce servings.

2: Pouring yogurt through a funnel helps avoid spills when containers have narrow necks. Use any clean bottle with a neck wide enough for a spoon to be used for scooping out yogurt after it has set. The bottle should be equipped with a cap.

3: Your oven can be used as a yogurt-maker if it will hold a temperature setting of 105 to 112F steadily for several hours. If the oven heat goes above 115F, it may kill the bacteria whose actions make the yogurt ferment.

Fresh-Fruit Yogurt

1 quart fresh milk
2 tablespoons powdered milk
½ cup fresh fruit or berries
1 tablespoon plain, unflavored
    commercial yogurt
Honey to taste

Scald fresh and powdered milk and cool to 110F. Incubate as directed for Basic Yogurt, and then mix in remaining ingredients. Refrigerate to chill before serving.
    Makes four 9-ounce servings.

Yogurt Salad Dressing

1 cup Basic Yogurt
⅓ cup apple-cider vinegar
1 medium onion, minced
⅔ cup safflower oil
1 clove garlic, minced
½ cup chopped celery leaves
¼ cup chopped parsley leaves

Blend all ingredients in an electric blender until smooth.
    Makes 2½ cups.

Yogurt Tomato Soup

4 cups tomato juice
2 cups Basic Yogurt
Pinch tarragon, preferably fresh
Lemon twists (optional)

Blend tomato juice, yogurt, and tarragon in an electric blender until smooth. Serve cold. Garnish each serving with a twist of lemon, if desired.
    Makes 6 servings.

Yogurt Cream Cheese

2 cups Basic Yogurt
1 pinch sea salt
Minced chives, green onions, herbs,
    or savory seeds to taste; or
    fresh-fruit slices (optional)

Pour surface whey from yogurt. Mix in sea salt, and put yogurt into a bag made of three 12-by-18-inch layers of cheesecloth. Hang bag over sink, and let drain overnight, or until yogurt is consistency of cream cheese. Refrigerate. If desired, add one of optional flavorings before serving as a spread. For a sweet flavor, blend or serve with fresh-fruit slices. For a sharper cheese, use yogurt several days old.
    Makes 2 cups.

Making Sour Cream

Now that you have made several fermented dishes, you might like to try sour cream, which also depends on fermentation but uses a buttermilk culture instead of yogurt bacteria. Try sweetened sour cream with fresh fruits and fruit salad: Into 1 cup of sour cream stir 1 tablespoon of granulated sugar. Plain sour cream (2 cups) mixed with 1 small garlic clove, minced, makes a delicious dip for potato chips.

Sour Cream

1 pint fresh dairy heavy cream
5 teaspoons commercial cultured
    buttermilk

Thoroughly mix the cream and the buttermilk. (Shake buttermilk container well before measuring.) Pour mixture into a container that allows an inch or two of space at the top. Cover tightly, and shake thoroughly. Let stand in a warm place (70 to 85F) for 24 hours. Or improvise an incubator, as in photograph 4. Refrigerate. Serve cold.
    Makes 1 pint.

4: Incubator for sour cream is improvised from potful of warm water and thick, warm blanket. Place container of buttermilk and fresh cream mixture in the warm water, and set pot on several thicknesses of the blanket. Wrap the rest of the blanket around pot and container, and leave overnight to incubate.

Cheeses

There are many legends about the discovery of cheesemaking, most of them with elements in common: Someone sets out on horseback on a journey, taking along some milk in a pouch made from a calf's stomach. After some time, the traveler discovers that the milk has turned into a palatable sour curd.

Rennin, an enzyme from the lining of a calf's stomach, converts milk into curds and whey and is used almost universally in cheesemaking. The chief milk protein, casein, is curdled, or coagulated, by the enzyme action of rennet or pepsin, or by lactic acid produced by bacterial action, or by a combination of these.

Cheese is made from the milk of various animals, including cow, sheep, goat, buffalo, camel, ass, mare, llama, reindeer, yak, and zebu. As with yogurt, the flavor and consistency of cheese are determined by the type of milk and the conditions under which it is converted. And like wine, cheese has countless varieties. Basically, it is either soft or hard. Soft cheeses generally contain more moisture than hard cheeses. The homemaker can easily make soft cheeses, many of which have a cottage-cheese base. The recipe on the opposite page is a good takeoff point.

Making Cottage Cheese

Soft cheeses such as cottage cheese can be made with rennet, yogurt, or cultured buttermilk as a starter. The recipe opposite uses rennet. This can

Before there were dairy trucks, milk vendors dispensed their product in city streets, from pails, as shown in this sketch of a milkman of the 1820s.

5: Cheesecloth bag twisted at the top serves as a press to force out watery, sour whey after the rennet-set milk curds have been heated.

6: Shifting curds around by lifting the corners of the cheesecloth after whey has been removed loosens them so water can rinse through the curds in next step.

7: Loosened curds in their cheesecloth bag are dipped in cold water and then drained as shown here. The cheesecloth around them is not squeezed.

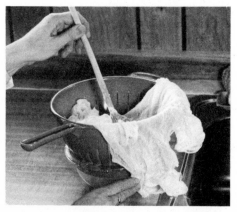

8: Back in the colander after their water bath, the curds are gently worked with a wooden spoon to loosen and lighten the mass. Cottage cheese is now ready to eat.

be purchased as junket rennet tablets, from Salada Foods, Inc., 399 Washington Street, Woburn, Mass. 01801, or as Hansen's cheese rennet tablets, from C. Hansen's Laboratories, 9015 West Maple Street, Milwaukee, Wis. 53214. A grocery store in your area may stock junket tablets; some pharmacies sell Hansen's; but both are usually difficult to obtain except from the manufacturers.

Basic Cottage Cheese

¹/₆ Hansen's cheese rennet tablet, or
  2 junket rennet tablets
¼ cup cold water

2 quarts skim milk
⅛ cup commercial cultured buttermilk

Dissolve the tablet in the cold water. Combine skim milk and buttermilk. Heat milk mixture to 70F. Add rennet solution, and stir well. Cover with a towel, and let stand at room temperature 12 to 18 hours, or until a smooth curd forms. With a long knife, cut the curd into ½-inch pieces. Slowly heat curds, in a double-boiler top over hot water, until temperature reaches 110F. Keep at this temperature 20 to 30 minutes, stirring about every 5 minutes so curds heat uniformly. When curds are firm, pour into a colander lined with cheesecloth, and let the whey drain off. Shift curds around by gently lifting the corners of the cloth. After whey has drained off, draw corners of cloth together, and immerse for about 2 seconds in cold water. Work curds with a wooden spoon to free them of any excess whey. Stir; chill.

    Makes 8 servings

Coeur a la Creme—Heart of Cream—is shown with the heart-shape wicker basket traditionally used to drain and mold this classic French dessert.

A Cheese-Based Dessert

A delicious and simple dessert called Coeur a la Creme—Heart of Cream—can be made with Yogurt Cream Cheese, page 53, or Basic Cottage Cheese, above. Any fresh fruit may be used to garnish it. It is molded in a heart-shape basket.

Coeur a la Creme

4 cups homemade cream cheese or
  cottage cheese
1 cup Basic Yogurt

2 tablespoons granulated sugar
1 pint fresh berries, sliced
Granulated sugar to taste

Stir cheese, at room temperature, with yogurt and 2 tablespoons sugar until smooth. Line heart-shape basket with cheesecloth; set on soup plate. Pack mixture into basket; drain and chill several hours, or overnight. To serve, unmold; garnish with berries; sprinkle with sugar to taste.

    Makes 8 servings.

Cottage-Cheese Dip

2 cups homemade cottage cheese
1 teaspoon celery seeds
1 teaspoon dill seeds
1 teaspoon caraway seeds

1 teaspoon minced parsley
1 teaspoon minced chives
Pinch paprika

Blend cottage cheese with celery, dill, and caraway seeds. Add parsley and chives. Chill for several hours. Before serving, sprinkle lightly with paprika. Serve with crackers or bread rounds.

    Makes 2 cups.

Making Hard Cheese

Hard cheeses usually travel better and last longer than soft cheeses, but they are more complex and time-consuming to make. Most people, except the adventurous, will not bother with home preparation. But if you would like to try making hard cheese, the recipe on page 56 is a basic one. When you are making hard cheese, remember that Marco Polo brought cheese similar to this one from the Orient to Europe. In the days before refrigeration and rapid transportation, it was one of the staple foods for long-distance travelers, because it was nutritive, kept well, and was easily carried.

Basic Process for Hard Cheese

The basic process for making hard cheese is similar to that for soft cheese, but hard cheeses are usually made in large batches because they keep well and are aged several weeks before use. The recipe below makes a single pound cheese. By doubling proportions, you can make a cheese twice the size. John Leland, a Cheshire, Mass., cheesemaker, presented President Jefferson with a cheese weighing 1,235 pounds—which is to say you can make hard cheese in very large sizes.

If you plan to make hard cheese often, you will want to have a cheese press. A simple one for small cheeses can be constructed from two 8-by-12-inch pieces of ¾-inch board, sanded. Join them with two 1-inch dowels, one centered through each end. With the lump of fresh cheese on the lower board, press the top board down, flattening the cheese evenly as you press out the remaining whey. As a substitute, set the cheese on a large, clean plate; set another plate on top, and weight—with an iron, for instance.

Hard cheese is coated with paraffin or oil before its aging period.

Basic Hard Cheese

2 gallons fresh milk (preferably raw)	1 cup cold water
¾ Hansen's cheese rennet tablet, or 8 junket rennet tablets	2 tablespoons sea salt

Let 1 gallon of the milk ripen overnight in a cool place (50 to 60F). The following morning, add the other gallon. In a large, enamel or stainless-steel pot, warm the milk to 86F. Add tablet to the cold water, and stir until dissolved. Set pot in a larger vessel of warm water (88 to 90F), away from drafts. Add rennet solution, and stir thoroughly. Let stand undisturbed until a firm curd forms—about 30 to 45 minutes. Test firmness by carefully putting a finger into the curd at an angle and lifting it. If curd breaks cleanly over your finger, it is ready to cut. If not, let it set 15 to 20 minutes longer.

Remove pot from larger vessel, and cut curd into ⅜-inch cubes. Use a knife with a blade long enough to cut through to bottom of pot without the handle's touching the curd. Stir curd cubes carefully but thoroughly with wooden spoon about 15 minutes; use long, slow movements so curds are not crushed. Place pot in a larger pot with water (creating a double-boiler effect), and heat slowly, raising curds' temperature about 1½ degrees every 5 minutes until it reaches 102F. Stir with a wooden spoon to keep curds from sticking together. Remove from heat when curds start to hold their shape and readily fall apart when held, but not squeezed, together.

Stir every 5 minutes for about 1 hour (that's right!) to keep curds from sticking. Leave them in the whey until the mass becomes so firm that a handful of pieces, pressed together, will shake apart easily. Put the curds on a double layer of 3-foot-square cheesecloth, and pull corners of cloth together. Swing gently, letting curds roll back and forth so whey drains without squeezing. Sprinkle curds with half of sea salt, and mix well with wooden spoon. Sprinkle on remaining sea salt, and mix in by hand.

Tie cheesecloth so curds form a ball; hang up, and let whey drip for 45 minutes. Remove cheesecloth; fold it into a rectangular bandage, 3 inches by 3 feet, and wrap tightly around the ball. With your hands, press down on ball until top and bottom are flat. Put three or four layers of cheesecloth under and over the cheese. Place in press; adjust pieces of wood; put a heavy object on the press; leave overnight. Turn; press overnight again.

Remove cheese from the press, and remove cheesecloth wrapping. Let stand in a warm room (70 to 75F) for 6 hours while rind forms and dries out. Then coat with hot, melted paraffin. Holding cheese with tongs, dip one half and then the other. Or paint on paraffin with a basting brush. An alternate to paraffin coating is rubbing vegetable oil into the cheese. Ripen in a cool place (50 to 65F) 3 to 4 weeks; turn two or three times a week.

Makes about one pound of cheese.

9: Test curd for hard cheese to see if it is firm enough. If curd slides down your finger instead of breaking cleanly over it, let curd set longer.

10: Cut curds with a long-bladed knife. Note that the pieces of curd here are quite small, about ⅜ inch in size. As you cut, avoid crushing the curds.

11: Place curds in the center of a double layer of cheesecloth; then pull cloth corners together to form a cradle, and roll curds in it gently.

Churning   ¢ ☒ 👪 🪣

Churning or agitating is the process that makes fat globules in milk unite—the end product is butter. The process dates back to about 2000 B.C., when churning was achieved by filling skin pouches with milk and throwing them back and forth or letting them swing over the backs of trotting horses. The butter made then was used most often as an ointment for the bath, a medicine or an illuminating oil.

As butter became a staple food, hand churns for the dairy were devised—rotating, swinging, or rocking barrels or boxes and cylindrical vessels equipped with plungers or dashers. Today, butter is made with electric churns. Churning time depends on the composition of the butterfat; the temperature, acidity, and richness of the cream; the speed and motion of the churn; and the size of the fat globules.

Butter's natural color, which ranges from pale yellow to deep gold, is derived from the carotene in the fodder the milk-giving animal—the cow or some other animal—has eaten. In the United States, cream from cow's milk is generally used in making butter; but in other countries, cream from the milk of goats, sheep, and mares is converted into butter.

All butter, when it is freshly made, is sweet. Salt is added to butter as a preservative and for flavor. You can easily make your own fresh, sweet butter using an electric mixer. When heavy cream is whipped long enough, it is transformed into little round, yellow globules of fat swimming in a bowl of whey. When it is beaten for another minute or so, the grainy, yellow lumps join together to form a ball of butter.

You can follow the recipe below to make a variety of flavored butters. Just beat in honey or salt to taste, or add herbs, spices, or other flavorings.

Flavored Butter

½ pint heavy cream   ½ to 1 teaspoon salt, herbs,
                                        spices, or other flavorings

In a medium bowl whip cream with an electric mixer at medium speed until butter separates from whey. Pour off whey; beat in flavoring.
    Makes ¼ pound.

Making Fresh Mayonnaise

A churning process with a different principle behind it produces a delicious fresh mayonnaise. By beating mustard into the yolks of eggs, along with a bit of salt and a little vinegar or lemon juice, you create a chemical change that allows the yolks to absorb quantities of oil, rather as rice absorbs water when it is boiled. The result is a creamy, golden mayonnaise with a unique flavor. It is an excellent dressing for meat salads, cold vegetables, and potato salad. Sweetened with 1 teaspoon granulated sugar and mixed half and half with whipped cream, it is delicious with jellied salad rings.

Mayonnaise

1 teaspoon salt   2 tablespoons vinegar or lemon juice
½ teaspoon dry mustard   1½ cups salad oil
2 egg yolks   Pinch cayenne

In a medium bowl, mix salt, mustard, egg yolks, and 1 teaspoon vinegar. With electric mixer at high speed, beat in ¼ of the oil, a few dribbles at a time. Add the remaining vinegar and the cayenne. Slowly beat in the remaining oil. Keep refrigerated.
    Makes 1¾ cups.

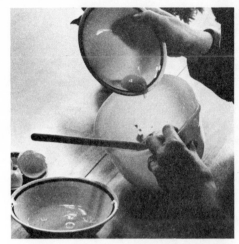

12: Adding egg yolks to salt and mustard is first step in making fresh mayonnaise. Stir mixture with a wooden spoon until the ingredients form a smooth paste. Then stir in 1 teaspoon of the vinegar.

13: With electric mixer at high speed, beat the egg mixture while dribbling in ¼ of the oil, a few drops at a time. Next, beat in remaining vinegar; then slowly dribble in remaining oil.

14: Garnish with a few tarragon leaves, and the finished mayonnaise is ready to be served. It has a rich golden color and a thick, creamy texture and holds its shape like whipped cream.

CLAMBAKES

The Ultimate Cookout

North American Indians were having clambakes before the first settlers from Europe reached New England. The Indians cooked their clams, corn and other food, much as many New England clambakers have done, in pits about 2 feet deep lined with stones. First a fire was built on the stones to heat them, and damp seaweed was placed on the hot stones to produce steam. Then the food was placed on the seaweed and more seaweed was placed on the food. Cooking time using this traditional method was 8 to 10 hours, a tribute to the patience of the Indians and early settlers.

Another clambake cooking method involves digging a pit in the sand, burying a large barrel almost to the top in the pit, and adding a small amount of water to the barrel. Stones heated in a separate fire are then put in the barrel, followed by successive layers of seaweed and food until the barrel is full. A tarp is tied down over the barrel top, which is then covered with sand. Cooking time using this method is only a few hours, but it takes a long time to dig the pit and heat the stones.

The clambake technique popular today substitutes for the pit or barrel a sheet of steel about 4 by 8 feet, set on rock or cinder-block supports built 1½ to 2 feet above ground. A wood fire heats the steel sheet, and layers of seaweed and food are placed on the steel, and then covered with a tarp. Cooking takes about an hour and the setup can feed dozens of people easily, making it ideal for club, neighborhood or community groups. Dividing the costs of the structural ingredients over a large group also makes such clambakes more palatable financially. The edible ingredients (lobsters, clams, corn, potatoes, onions, chicken and hotdogs) will be costly enough today.

Formerly a florist, Bill Foster began organizing clambakes for friends and summer visitors in his York Harbor, Me. backyard more than 22 years ago. More recently Foster, and his wife Phoebe, have been wintering in Key Biscayne, Fla. where they prepare bakes. The highlight of Foster's career was a special party prepared for then–First Lady, Mrs. Lyndon Johnson.

At left, a hungry crowd watches as canvas tarp is taken off, signaling that the food is ready. Above, nestled on a bed of seaweed is the menu prior to cooking: Hotdogs, clams, corn, lobsters, Bermuda onions, potatoes. String attached to test potato, lets cook pull it out to check on cooking progress.

Notes for a Small Clambake

If you want to serve up to eight people, you can use a large enamel pot, and cook over a stove or barbecue grill at home, or take the pot to a picnic area where grills are available. (You can also buy a clam steamer at hardware stores in areas where clambakes are popular. These large pots come in 16 or 20 quart sizes, have two separate compartments for the food, and a spigot at the bottom for draining off the clam juice and water.) If you use a large pot, line its bottom with a couple of inches of seaweed and add a quart of water. Place a test potato close to the edge of the pot where it won't disturb the other food ingredients when you pull it out. Add the rest of the food in the same order you would for a large bake and pack seaweed around the top and sides of the inside of the pot. Then cover and cook until the test potato tells you the food is done. Combine the broth of water and clam juice with melted butter to make a dip or spread for the food.

There are no rigid rules for having a clambake. Small groups of 6 to 8 people can enjoy a feast of clams, corn, potatoes, onions and lobsters, steamed in large kettles as explained in the text at left. Groups of several dozen or more will need a larger cooking setup, similar to the above-ground "pit" shown on page 58. This is particularly true if the group wants a more elaborate meal, including chicken, hotdogs and, perhaps, some local food specialty such as conch.

A good cooking site for the above-ground pit would be a graveled backyard space, an empty lot or a beach area, if the owner's permission can be obtained by your club or community group. To build the pit, you will need 16 cement cinder blocks (or an equivalent volume of rocks), and a 4 by 8 foot sheet of steel (or a discarded car hood with its paint and grease burned off). For holding the food while it cooks, build a bin consisting of a 2½ by 3½ by 1 foot scrap wood frame with a hardware cloth bottom. A 4 by 5 foot canvas tarp, a smaller section of tarp to tuck around the food in the bin, enough rope to tie the large tarp down over the food bin, a bucket for water used to dampen the seaweed and tarp, a kettle for melting butter, containers for carrying food, an apron, work gloves (to protect against heat and lobsters), and a pitchfork complete the list of cooking accessories needed for clambaking. In addition, for each bake, you will need: about ¼ cord of dry wood and some newspapers to help start the wood burning; and about 3 bushels of wetted-down seaweed. (Corn husks, long grass, Irish moss, palmetto leaves or other plants can be used instead.) You will also need small cheesecloth bags (available from hardware stores) to hold your clams and the two test potatoes you will use to show you when the food is ready.

Calculating Food Portions

Then, of course, there is the all-important food. For each adult guest at a typical clambake, plan on serving: 1 pint of clams; 1 lobster and/or ½ chicken; 1 or 2 ears of corn; 1 or 2 potatoes; 1 or 2 hotdogs; a couple of small onions; and ½ cup of butter or margarine. If you think the guests will have room for dessert (and they usually do) add watermelons to your shopping list. And don't forget the liquid refreshments; seafood and open-air cooking can raise quite a thirst. To serve the food, you will need sturdy, non-absorbent paper plates, large heat-resistant paper cups for the clams and small ones for the melted butter, plenty of napkins, and hand-sized rocks for each guest to use for cracking the lobsters open.

To set up the pit, line up the cinder blocks in two parallel rows about

1: The walls of the bake "pit" can be made with cinder blocks (above) or large stones can be used if they are available. Walls should stand 1½ to 2 feet high.

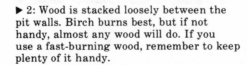

▶ 2: Wood is stacked loosely between the pit walls. Birch burns best, but if not handy, almost any wood will do. If you use a fast-burning wood, remember to keep plenty of it handy.

3: Sixteen-year-old Mark Foster gathers Maine rockweed (a form of seaweed) shortly before the bake. But you need not live in Maine to enjoy your steamers. In other parts of the country, use other greenery.

4: First layer on top of sheet-metal is rockweed, spread 6 to 8 inches deep. Whatever greenery you find to use, make sure it is thoroughly wet down for clambake.

5: The four-sided wood and hardware cloth bin is placed on the seaweed. If you are serving only a small number of people— say, six—bin isn't necessary.

4 feet apart, photograph 1. If you use rocks instead of blocks, make sure they are stacked to a height of 1½ to 2 feet. Between these walls, loosely pile your firewood to a height of about 1 foot, as shown in photograph 2; this will leave space for the fire to breathe. Lay the steel sheet on top of the two block walls, as in photograph 4. Spread a 6- to 8-inch deep layer of wet seaweed on top of the metal sheet. Then center the food bin on top of the seaweed, photograph 5. Place two test potatoes, each in a separate cheese-cloth bag, at diagonally opposite corners on the wire bottom of the bin. Make sure the strings attached to each bag are long enough to trail down over the sheet metal's edge, so that you can reach them comfortably.

Since the bottom of the bin will be hottest, the foods that normally take the longest to cook make up the first or bottom layer you put in the bin. For

7: Properly placed in the bin, the food is ready for baking. Note clams in cheesecloth bags, and string in lower left corner leading from test potato.

8: Because of abundance of ingredients stacked in the bin to feed more than a dozen people, Foster uses small canvas tarp to keep food from scattering.

9: Another 2 to 3 inches more seaweed on top of the small tarp helps retain the heat and moisture. Now the fire can be started, and steam will begin to generate.

6: Mark Foster adds corn ears, still in their husks, to the trough. Ingredients requiring the longest baking times go in first; those that cook quickly, last.

this particular bake, that means that the potatoes and Bermuda onions go in first. Next comes the chicken (cut in half and thoroughly defrosted if purchased whole or frozen). Next are the lobsters, and then the corn (still in its husks), together with the hotdogs. The clams, dropped into cheesecloth bags to keep them from being scattered among the other foods, make up the final layer in the bin. If you are baking for a large group and your food bin is tightly packed, it may help to tuck the food snugly into its bin with a small tarp. This will help hold the food in its bin and keep it separated from the seaweed. It will also help contain heat and moisture. But the small tarp is optional. Whether or not you use the extra tarp, you should cover the food (or small tarp) with a layer of seaweed, about 2 to 3 inches deep. Then top this final layer of seaweed with a tarp large enough to be tied down around the food bin to help retain the moisture and heat.

Light Your Fire
With the food bin filled and the large, outer tarp tied over it, you can light your fire and let the cooking begin. Make sure your bucket of water is handy; the fire will dry out your weeds and tarp so they need re-wetting in order to keep the steam generating. And it is the steam that does the cooking. The clams will open after some 20 minutes of steaming. That's when they start letting their savory juices seep down over the foods below them, giving the meal its distinctive clambake flavor.

Hungry though you may be, you must wait from 40 to 60 minutes after your fire is well under way for the food to be ready. The precise time will depend on how hot the fire is and how much food you are cooking. That's why you have the two test potatoes. After 40 or 50 minutes, pull out one of the test potatoes; if it crushes easily, your bake is done. If it is still hard, wait until 10, 20 or even 30 more minutes have passed (depending on how hard the first potato was), and then try the second test potato. It should be done; if not, allow a little more cooking time before you serve the food. It is important that you keep the fire up and the steam generating from the seaweed throughout the cooking process.

10: A second, larger canvas tarp, wetted down, is tossed over the trough and weeds. Anchored with rope to pit base, it keeps steam from dissipating too quickly, thus conserving firewood.

11: The fire kept burning briskly and seaweed occasionally wet down as it dries, this clambake should be ready to eat in about an hour. For this particular bake, pit walls built up of locally available stones were used.

Serving the Bake

Just a few minutes before you expect the food to be done, put your butter or margarine in a kettle and set the kettle on the edge of the metal sheet, as in photograph 12. The melted butter will be used with the clams, lobsters, potatoes and corn. Then, as soon as a test potato indicates all is ready, serve the food as quickly as possible. Food—particularly clams—served in

12: Begin melting butter at sheet-metal edge a few minutes before you expect bake to be done. Melted butter can be poured from kettle into paper cups.

13: Pull test potato from bin after 40 or 50 minutes. If it crumbles easily, bake is ready. If not, cook another 10 or 20 minutes and try the second test potato.

When the lobsters have turned brilliant scarlet in color, it is another useful sign that the bake is ready for eating.

the open air cools rapidly. The assembly-line method of serving works well, with all the corn in one pan or basket, all the potatoes in another, all the onions in another, and so forth. The clams can be served directly out of their cheesecloth bags.

Self-Service Lineup Best

Have the guests line up with paper plates in hand and help themselves to the corn, potatoes, chicken, onions, lobsters and hotdogs. The clams can be put in large, heat-resistant paper cups and the melted butter in smaller ones. Pour the butter directly from the kettle you heated it in, to save a mess. Make sure everyone has hand-sized rocks; these will be used for cracking open the lobster shells. This method works amazingly well and is lots of fun, particularly for the younger guests. (But just to be on the safe side—if you think some of the guests will be fussy about how they eat their lobsters or will have difficulty with the rock crushing—it might be wise to have a few nutcrackers, pliers and lobster forks available for those who ask for them.)

Dessert should be simple and portable. As mentioned earlier, watermelon is a good choice, and it should be served just when the clambakers are recovering from their first course. The choice of beverages is up to you—whatever you think the majority of the group will prefer. If you plan to serve coffee after the feast, it can be made in advance and heated up on the metal sheet while the first course is underway.

This youngster agrees that watermelon makes an ideal dessert for a clambake. But other fruits may also be used.

14: Wear work gloves and take care in lifting steaming food from bin. Sort food by type in separate containers, from which guests can serve themselves.

15: A pitchfork will enable you to clear your steel sheet of hot weed which should be spread on the ground to cool. Weed can later be used as a fertilizer.

Cleaning Up

Once you've taken the baked food from the bin, lift the bin from its steaming weed bed. Be careful not to touch the hot metal hardware cloth or steel sheet. Use a pitchfork to lift the weed off the steel sheet. Spread the weed about on the ground so that it can cool quickly. Then reach under the sheet metal with the pitchfork, directly into the pit, and spread the wood and ashes as much as you can. By the time you've finished eating, the material you used to build your pit will be cool enough to handle.

Try to leave your bake area as clean and natural as you found it. This is especially important if you baked on a beach or lake shore. If you moved rocks to construct your pit base, scatter them again. With your pitchfork, scrape as much of the wood ash as you can into the sand or ground, and bury the charcoal. The weed you used can be saved for fertilizer or taken to the nearest dump or trash can along with the garbage that has accumulated. Obviously, your food bin, sheet-metal, tarps, and cement cinder blocks should be saved for your next big clambake.

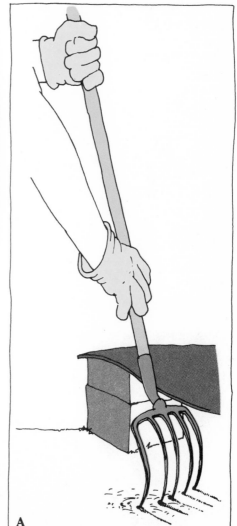

A

Figure A: Use pitchfork to scrape ashes into ground around the clambake site.

16: The clam's air hole is easily identified. Start to dig on one side of the hole and work your way toward it.

17: Crumble—don't rake—the wet sand with short, choppy strokes a few inches deep. Work your way past the hole.

18: As the rake churns up the sand, look for the clam, which can be anywhere within a few inches of its hole.

19: Place clam in a slat-bottomed trough. Continue to chop sand along the beach where siphon holes appear.

This fully-equipped clam digger walks toward a Maine beach with his tools in hand. Regulations for clamming vary in different localities but permits are required.

Clamming

Although you can order clams from your local fish or specialty food store, you might consider a clamming expedition to get you into a clambake mood. The edible clam most popular with those living along the Atlantic Coast is the soft-shell. It is also called the steamer or long-neck (because of its long siphon). Soft-shell clams are usually 2 to 4 inches in diameter, and have thick but brittle shells that are often chalky white but may be stained by the ground. The harder-shelled quahog or littleneck clams, found from southern Canada to Florida, are 4 to 5 inches in diameter when grown. They are grayish outside and whitish inside, usually with one deep purple edge. When small, they are known as cherrystone clams. Quahogs can be kept refrigerated for several weeks but soft-shell clams should be eaten promptly.

An edible clam found on both coasts is the razor clam, about 6 or 7 inches long and 1 inch across. Other West Coast favorites include the pismo and the large geoduck, which is considered a real delicacy.

The tools you will need for clamming are a clam rake and a slat-bottomed trough. Both are available at hardware stores near clamming areas. You will also need a permit for clamming, usually available at the local town hall. When you pick up the permit, ask where the best clam beds are, and whether any areas have been posted off-limits because of water pollution. Clams can be collected more easily when the tide is low. So also ask to see a tide table you can check for the best clamming times.

When you reach your clamming beach, look around for the telltale holes made by the clams' siphons. Each hole will be a deep indentation, about ½ inch in diameter, that stands out against the smooth beach. Dig the rake's teeth into the mud a few inches on your side of the hole and drag it toward you, crumbling the sand as you go. Work toward the hole, keeping a sharp eye out for the clam. When you find it, make sure it is regulation size, and, if it is, put it into your slat-bottomed trough. When you've dug your limit of clams, wash them by jiggling the trough around in the water. Then take them home to eat and remember that they're tastiest if cooked the same day.

▶ 20: When you've filled the trough, wash the sand clinging to the clams by dipping the container in the sea and gently agitating it. The rake and trough are the only tools needed and can be found in any hardware store in the clamming area. A bucket with holes punched through the bottom might be substituted for the clam trough.

▼ Clamming is done in the area of beach exposed by low tide, anywhere below the high water mark. It's backbreaking work and often takes hours, but the rewards are great. It's also messy, so wear old clothes and prepare to get very dirty. Before you start, be sure to check local regulations about permits and minimum clam size.

DOLLS AND DOLL CLOTHES
People For a Small World

There is something of magic in the making of a doll. With a few scraps of cloth, a piece of cardboard, and some glue, you can fashion a figure that acquires a personality of its own as you add a face and a hairdo. By the time you have put in the last stitches, given the doll a name, and placed it in the arms of a waiting child, the doll is ready to become a very real part of your household.

During the early years of U.S. history, when elaborate dolls were hard to come by, pioneer mothers made do with what was at hand, as the Indians had long been doing. They fashioned dolls from the husks of corn (page 74), and they used the shells of eggs (page 71) and nuts and fruits (pages 70 and 73) for heads. In the late 1800s, they used clothespins to make the kinds of dolls shown on page 72. Patterns for clothes for the dolls with walnut, egg, and dried-apple heads are on page 71. Many dolls like those from early days are still being made in the mountains of the eastern United States, where the old crafts continue to be practiced in traditional ways.

In the nineteenth century, bisque dolls and others of china like my great-grandmother's, pictured below, became available, particularly in urban areas. Today, many of them are in antique-doll collections. These dolls were expensive even in their day, and techniques for repairing them developed. Some of these techniques are given in the Craftnotes, on page 75.

Margaret Perry is Travel and Craft Editor of Early American Life *magazine. Her travels have taken her far from her native Connecticut in her search for historic sites and early crafts, both here and abroad. She is the author of* Christmas Magic, Rainy Day Magic, *and* Christmas Card Magic.

▲ This 1830 doll belonged to Peg Perry's great-grandmother, who learned to sew by making the doll wardrobe that is kept in the miniature trunk.

◄ Dollmaking techniques from Colonial days produced this collection of 3- to 6-inch charmers. Instructions for making each doll—with a dried apple, walnut, cloth pieces, cornhusk, or eggs—are given on the following pages.

Walnut and egg dolls

1: Glue white yarn for hair to walnut in a continuous spiral. Use a toothpick to spread white glue across the shell joint. Hold yarn in place until glue dries.

2: Draw facial features with a fine-pointed black felt pen. The features should be small and delicate. Practice drawing them on spare walnuts.

3: Secure pipe-cleaner arms to cone with masking tape. Crisscross the tape over the shoulder area. This will give additional shape to the top of the cone.

4: Wrap arms with cotton batting. Tie it firmly at the wrists to prevent slipping. Dress sleeves will fit over the cotton. The arms can be bent to any position.

The materials you will need for one walnut-head doll are: an English walnut (any size); a 14-inch square of light cardboard; a pipe cleaner, 7 inches long; a yard of white yarn; strips of cotton batting; masking tape; a felt pen; white glue; ⅛ yard of calico for dress and bonnet.

For the hairdo, glue the yarn to one side of the nut in a continuing spiral (photograph 1); start where the halves of the shell come together. Cover the back of the head with this spiraled yarn.

The shell joint makes a perfect nose for the doll. With a fine-pointed black felt pen (photograph 2), draw four curved lines for eyebrows and eyelids; make two large dots for eyes, two tiny dots (one on each side of the joint) for the nose, and a tiny slightly upcurving line for the mouth.

The doll's body is a cardboard cone 6 inches high. On the square of flexible cardboard, draw a circle 12 inches in diameter. From this, cut out a quarter section, and bend it into a cone. Fasten edges together with masking tape. Cut half an inch off the point, so the walnut will sit easily on top of the cone. Glue the walnut head to the cone.

Cut or punch a small hole in each side of the cone near the top; put the pipe cleaner through the holes, to make arms; secure with tape (photograph 3). Wrap cotton around arms for thickness and to hold clothing (photograph 4).

Following the patterns on the opposite page, cut out skirt, bodice, sleeves, and bonnet. Sew seams, and sew sleeves to bodice. Gather skirt at waist. The dress can be sewed or glued on; the bonnet is glued to the head.

The bodies and clothes for the egg-head dolls pictured on the opposite page are made the same way.

Three walnut-head gossips stand chatting on a shelf in an antique corner cupboard. Natural variations in the walnut shells and in the hand-drawn features give each doll a unique character, although all were made the same way.

5: With the fine point of small, sharp scissors, make a tiny hole in each end of the eggshell. Then blow into one hole. This will expel the contents.

Eggshells are an especially good shape to form the heads of dolls dressed in calico and gingham. The hair of the doll wearing the bonnet is done in a bun.

To make an egg-head doll, you need the same materials, except that you use an egg for the head and need 2 or 4 yards of yellow or light-brown yarn; some ribbon, a red felt marker or rouge. Start by blowing out the egg (photograph 5).

To make pigtails, glue 12 strands of yarn 12 inches long across the top of the head, starting just at the forehead and continuing down the back. Make two braids (photograph 6), and tie on ribbons matching the dress fabric. To make a bun, use 6-inch strands of yarn; glue on the same way, but fold up the ends and tie them into a bun with thread.

Draw the doll's face with a fine-pointed black felt pen. Put a touch of color on the lips and cheeks with a red felt marker or rouge.

6: When the yarn has been glued to the head, divide it into two sets of six strands, and braid the pigtails. Tie on ribbon bows, and trim pigtail ends.

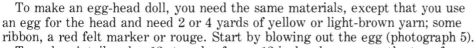
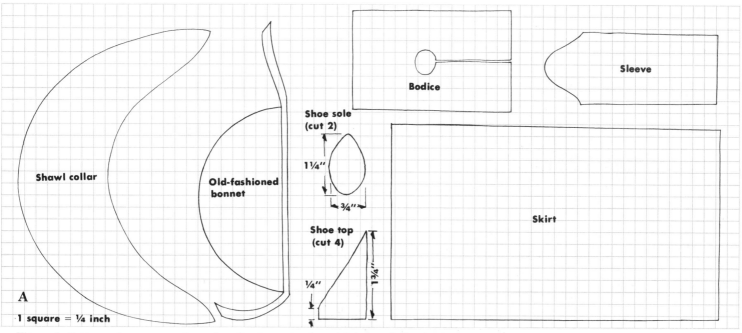

Shawl collar

Old-fashioned bonnet

Shoe sole (cut 2)

1¼"

¾"

Shoe top (cut 4)

¼"

1¾"

Bodice

Sleeve

Skirt

A

1 square = ¼ inch

Figure A: Patterns for costumes for walnut-head, egg-head, and dried-apple-head dolls. To enlarge, see page 158.

The traditional Indian pieces doll, a favorite with the Sioux Indians of South Dakota, does not have a face. Scraps of any size can be used to make these dolls. They stand, held up by the bunching of the fabric they are made of.

Pieces doll

This traditional Indian doll is made entirely of scraps of material—hence its name. The size depends on the size of the scraps. To make one like those pictured at left, you will need pieces of white and colored material, white glue, a safety pin, and string or strong thread.

First, roll a 6-inch square of white cloth into a ball, to make the head. Drape a 6-inch square of white cloth over this, for the body; tie it around the neck with thread. Next, drape a folded piece of dark cloth (slightly smaller than the white) over the head; tie it at the neck as well.

The dress can be crudely cut from a 3-by-6-inch piece of fabric folded into a square. Cut each side up at a slight angle toward the fold; then out to the edge, to make sleeves. Sew the side seams. Cut a hole in the fold for the doll's head. The cloak is a 5-inch square of fabric, folded to make a rectangle and fastened horizontally with a safety pin. No edges are finished except the dress hem, and this can be sewed or glued.

Making pieces dolls is a popular activity for children's parties.

7: For the head covering of the pieces doll, here seen from the front, fold a square of dark fabric, and tie it around the neck. Material helps form the body.

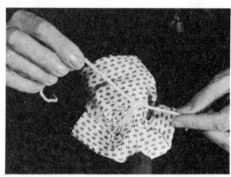

8: Tie the simple dress at the waist. Side seams are sewed, but the hem of the dress shown here is glued. This back view shows the doll's dark head covering.

Miniature home-made dolls, such as this clothespin doll held by five-year-old Ursina Amsler, have tremendous appeal for your children.

Clothespin doll

The materials needed to make a clothespin doll are: a wooden clothespin; a handful of polyester fiber filling or absorbent cotton; three ¼-by-4-inch strips of nylon; a ½-inch-wide strip of lacy nylon; a pipe cleaner, 4 inches long; a 3-by-8-inch piece of calico; a 3-by-8-inch piece of crinoline; string.

Pad the rounded top of the clothespin with ⅛-inch-thick polyester fiber or cotton. Cover the padded head with a nylon strip (cut from a slip or light-color hose), and tie the strip around the neck with string. Next, pad the chest area with polyester ¼-inch thick. Cover this padding with another nylon strip, and tie the strip around the waist. For the arms, wrap a pipe cleaner with a third nylon strip, and sew it horizontally to the center of the doll's back. Crisscross the chest area with a strip of lacy nylon, to form the blouse. Sew the blouse pieces securely at the waist.

The full skirt is stiffened with an underskirt of crinoline. Gather both the calico and the crinoline at the waist (the 8-inch sides), and sew tightly to the doll. Trim the crinoline and hem the skirt so that they just cover the bottom of the clothespin. The fabric holds the doll upright. Glue yarn to the head to make an attractive hairpiece, and use a felt-tip pen to color the lips and eyes.

Apple-head doll

To make an apple-head doll, you will need: a firm apple; two cloves; four tiny simulated pearls; yarn; ¼ yard of calico; black felt for shoes; scraps of silk for reticule; felt for hat; strips of cotton sheet; 6 feet of 14-gauge wire; cotton; white glue; rouge; clear lacquer; white thread; a tiny feather. Pare the apple; remove a small wedge on each side of the nose. Cut out ¼-inch holes for eye sockets. Make a curved slit, ¾-inch long, for the mouth. Push a clove into each eye socket (photograph 9). Embed the pearls in the mouth slit for teeth. Shape a 12-inch piece of 14-gauge wire and insert it through the head (photograph 10), leave a loop at the top and hang the apple from it to dry. The ends of the wire, extending from the neck, will later be used to attach head to body. Mold the apple features daily while it dries. In about a week, lacquer the apple and rouge lips and cheek. Make a T-shaped armature (photograph 11) from about 5 feet of wire, with arms 5, neck 1, legs 8 inches long. The wire goes down and up one leg, then the other, out to form an arm, across to the other arm and back. Twist where wires meet, to form the body. Wrap with strips of sheet tied with thread. Twist together body and head wires. Glue on enough yarn hair to show under the hat. Patterns for costume and black felt shoes are on page 71. Glue the two triangular top sections at the instep and center of the heel. Glue on the oval sole. Make the hat from a 2-by-4 inch piece of felt; draw a 3-inch-diameter circle (brim) and, inside it, a 1½-inch diameter circle (crown top). Cut out. Glue both to a ½-inch-wide felt band. Glue on the feather. Make reticule from a 4-inch-diameter circle of silk. Stitch around the edge, fill with ball of cotton, draw the thread, and as the final step, tie it to the doll's hand.

This dried-apple-head doll was made by Margaret Tallardy of Southington, Conn., whose dolls are featured at many New England craft festivals and fairs.

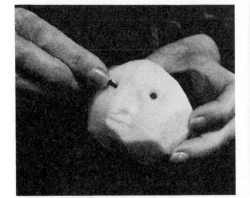

9: Place cloves in eye sockets after features have been carved in pared apple. When the apple is dry, put a dot of white paint in the center of each clove, or replace the cloves with buttons.

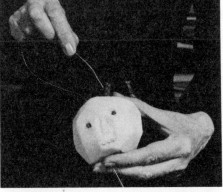

10: Push wire bent to U-shape through the core of the apple, from the top of the head to the neck. Leave a loop at the top for hanging the apple while it dries. Twist wire ends together at the neck.

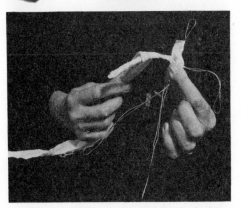

11: Pad the T-shape wire armature at the arms and chest to give the body form. Sew the clothes to this padded frame. Neck wire of armature is twisted with wires from the apple to join head to body.

73

Cornhusk doll

It is generally believed that the Indians taught early American settlers to make dolls of cornhusks, the outer covering on an ear of corn. Today, this is a popular craft project (see the light-blue cornhusk doll on page 68). You can dye cornhusks any color, as shown at left.

You will need husks from six ears of corn; dye or vegetable coloring; string; a 7-inch pipe cleaner; a black felt pen. Soak the husks in lukewarm water five minutes; leave them in the water while you make the doll. To make the head, tear off a ¼-inch-wide strip the full length of a husk, and roll it into a ball (photograph 12). Add more strips until the ball is ¾ inch in diameter. Pin, or tie in place with string. For the upper body, make a ball 1½ inches in diameter. To make arms, wind inch-wide strips around pipe cleaner (photograph 13); tie at the wrists with string or very narrow strips of husk.

To assemble head, arms, and upper body, start by draping a long, inch-wide piece of husk over the head (photograph 14). The inside of the husk should be on the outside; it makes a smoother face. Twist the ends to form a neck, and tie. Place the arms just under the neck, the upper body under the arms, and tie the husk below the upper body with string (photograph 15).

To make the skirt, place a layer of full-length husks, pointed ends up, around the waistline; tie securely. Add and tie husk layers until the skirt is very full, for this is what the doll stands on. Cut off husks evenly at the bottom. Add a bouffant overskirt if you like (photograph 16).

Make a bodice of two husk strips, ½ inch wide, crossed front and back and tied at the waist (photograph 17). Then cover the waistline with a ½-inch-wide husk sash, tied securely.

For hair, glue corn silk to the head. To make a bonnet, tie a 1-by-5-inch husk strip around head, and cut off excess. After doll has dried, draw facial features with a fine-pointed black felt pen. Sometimes only eyes and two tiny dots for the nose are drawn. If you draw a mouth, make it small.

Use your imagination to devise an umbrella from a pipe cleaner, or make a broom of twigs, for the cornhusk doll to carry.

Colored cornhusks show a few of the hues that can be achieved by dyeing. Use fabric dye that dissolves in cold water, and leave the husks in the bath for only a few minutes for a light tone, longer for a deeper shade. If you have vegetable coloring, you can use that to color cornhusks. You can work with the wet husks immediately after they have soaked in the coloring or dye. If they have dried out, soak them again in lukewarm water so you can shape them. Wet husks may be turned inside-out.

12: Roll cornhusk strips into balls to form the head and body. Secure each ball with a short straight pin or tie with string.

13: Wind inch-wide strips of husk around a pipe cleaner to form the arms. Arms can be bent even after husk dries.

14: Drape a strip of husk over head, long enough to cover arms and upper body. Secure it under the head with string.

15: Slip arms and an upper-body ball under the husk strip covering the head. Tie strip under the body ball, at waist.

16: To make a bouffant overskirt, tie husks at the waist, as shown; then let ends fall down over the string.

17: Add bodice husk strips and hide ends and skirt top with a 1/2-inch-wide sash. For security, use string to tie in waist.

DOLL CRAFTNOTES

In the nineteenth century, lifelike dolls with china or papier-mache heads were produced commercially. They were expensive toys. Unlike the expendable early Colonial dolls, they were too precious to discard when parts were damaged, and putting them back together again became an art.

The techniques developed then are used today, only a little updated. Some repairs—eye malfunctions, for instance—are best made at a doll hospital. Replacement parts can be purchased from many doll hospitals, collectors, and from mail order houses such as Yield House, North Conway, N.H., 04860; Mark Farmer Company, Inc., 36 Washington Avenue, Point Richmond, Calif. 94801; Jennifer House, Great Barrington, Mass. 01320; Old Guilford Forge, Guilford, Conn. 06437; Irma's Dolls, Route No. 2, Rome, Ohio 44805; Sullivan's, New Market, Md., 21774.

You can make new parts for a cloth body by adapting the principles used in the pattern, figure C, for Pauline Fischer's doll on pages 76 and 77. Or take the doll apart; make patterns from the parts; cut and sew them. Today, polyester fiber from the five-and-dime store is generally used as filling for cloth dolls.

Other problems easily repaired at home are these:

Lost eyelashes: Replace eyelashes with individual artificial lashes cut from those sold in strips at the beauty counters of drug stores. Lay the doll down, so its eyes close. With a toothpick, put a thread of white glue on one eyelid. With tweezers, place a single lash, and hold it until dry. Continue until lost lashes have been restored.

Cracks in finish: With a toothpick, smear the whole cracked area with a thin, smooth film of ceramic cement, sold at art-supply shops. As the cement begins to dry, press the edges of the crack firmly together, and hold until glue dries. It will dry clear, filling in the cracks.

Hair repair: Wigs suitable for dolls are sold in various sizes by doll hospitals in large cities. Before attaching a new wig, scrape off old glue, and wash the head with a cloth dampened in warm water. Wipe the head dry, and paint it with a thin coat of white glue. Position the wig, and hold it until the glue begins to set. After 24 hours, trim the wig to the desired length.

Limb joints: Jointed dolls that have become unstrung are easy to put together again, as shown in Figure B. To string a 12-inch doll, you will need one 12-inch and one 8-inch length of elastic. At each of the joints, there should be hooks for the elastic. If any of these hooks have been lost, fashion new ones from a 10-gauge wire; set into original holes; fill and seal in with ceramic cement.

Fasten the elastic to the hooks at the points shown in figure B. Center the elastic through the neck hook. Thread the ends through the body, out the leg openings, and pull the elastic to draw the head to the body. On the left side of the body, loop the elastic through the hook attached to the left leg. Then thread the left end back through the opening, across the body, and out through the right-leg opening. Loop the right end of the elastic through the right-leg hook. Knot the ends, making the knot larger than the eye of the hook.

To connect the doll's arms, center the 8-inch piece of elastic through the right-arm hook and pull both ends of the elastic through the body and out the left-arm hole. Pass one end through the left-arm hook and tie the ends together.

Irving Chais, owner of the New York Doll Hospital, in New York City, carries on the business his father founded in the early 1900s.

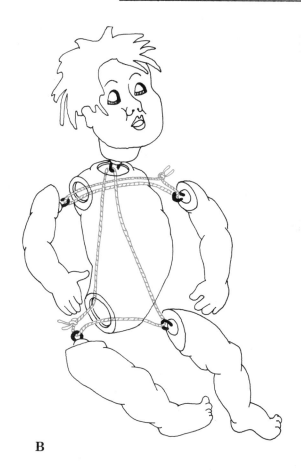

B

Figure B: To tie elastic, make a single overhand knot and pull the ends almost taut. Maintain this tension while you make a square knot. The elastic should pull arms, legs and head into place. Test joints by placing doll in sitting and standing positions. Then trim ends of elastic and tuck them inside the body.

Cloth doll

This old-fashioned doll was made by
Pauline Fischer 25 years ago for her
daughter. The original doll's body is made
of white muslin; face, arms and neck of
pink muslin; and the back of the head of
yellow muslin matching the yarn hair.
Instructions for the adaptation of the
doll, given in figure C, call for one
color of fabric, flesh-colored muslin.

Making this old-fashioned doll is a challenge because the pattern has so many
parts. You will need: a few strands of cotton embroidery floss, blue for the
irises of the eyes, light brown for the brows, nose, freckles, poppy red for
the mouth; two rounds of black felt for eye pupils; two skeins of cotton or
wool rug yarn (yellow) for the hair; a large bag of polyester fiber for the
filling; flesh-colored muslin or cotton, 1½ yards (36-inch width) or 1¼ yards
(45-inch width), for the covering. To give the doll a finished look, press
each seam open as it is completed, then turn it right side out and press again.

From figure C, prepare a paper pattern, following instructions on page
158. Transfer all notches and markings. Pattern pieces lettered (a)
are duplicates; two pieces of that number are required. Note that pattern
piece 4 requires four pieces. Using the pattern cut out the fabric pieces.

Embroidering the Face: On the face (piece 1) use satin stitch to embroider
brows, irises, mouth; use seed stitch to embroider freckles; use outline stitch
to embroider nose. See instructions for making these stitches in "Needlework
Sampler," pages 118 to 129. Sew down felt pupils cut to size you will achieve
when you have enlarged pattern piece 1.

Making the Head: With right sides of fabric facing, and double notches
matched, sew chin, 2, to face, 1. Cut back of head, 3, completely apart along
dashed interior lines. With right sides facing, stitch these pieces together
again, matching notches to give head contour. Match notches at forehead centers
of 1 and 3, and sew pieces together with right sides facing. Stop stitching
where chin begins. Turn right side out. Stuff head with polyester filling.

Making the Arms: With right sides facing, sew together two arm pieces
numbered 4. Right side out, stitch finger lines. Do not sew arm sockets closed.
On wrong side, pin 5 to 4, matching the notch on 5 to the shoulder-top seam
on 4. Sew 4 and 5 together on the three curved sides only, leaving a 1-inch
opening around the notch in 5. Turn right side out. With polyester filling,
stuff the arm full. Turn unsewn socket seam edges in, and handsew arm closed.
With right side facing, sew up long and short seams. Turn right side out.
Fold arm tab, 6, along the solid line. Tuck tab seam allowance into 1-inch
opening left in arm top and handstitch. Make the right arm in the same way
from pieces 4a, 5a, 6a.

Making the Body: With the right sides facing, use a double row of stitching
to sew together the shoulder sections of the body, front and back, 7 and 8.
Sew side sections 9, 9a, to 7 and 8, matching notches. Do not sew bottom
seams. Turn right side out. Pin bottom seams securely together.

With right sides facing, sew together the sides of neck front and back, 10
and 11. Turn right side out. Match notches on 10 and 11 to the notches in the
neck fronts of 7 and 8. On the right side, pin neck onto body, easing fabric
around curves. Sew together by hand. Stuff body.

Making Legs and Feet: With right sides facing, sew the leg front, 12, to
the vamp, 13, matching double notches. Sew 13 to 14, the sole, matching
single notches. Sew 15, leg back, to 12, leg front, easing the heel into the
sole. Turn leg right side out, stuff, and sew up the seam at the top of the
leg (photograph 18). Prepare the other leg and foot from 12a, 13a, 14a, 15a.
Unpin body seat bottom, pin leg tabs into place between bottom seams and sew
up with a double row of stitching.

Finishing the Doll: Ease head down over neck and adjust stuffing. Handstitch
into place around back with seam allowance turned in. Sew arm tabs securely
to body shoulder, stitching chin.

To make the doll's hair, cut 45 36-inch strands of wool, fold them in half
to make double 18-inch strands. At the fold, handstitch each strand to the
doll's head at the hairline, beginning and ending at points level with the
lower rim of her eyes (photograph 19). Trim the ends.

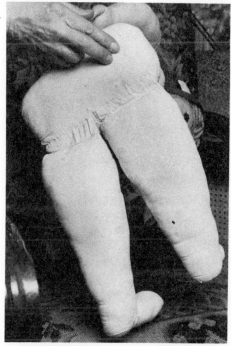

18: Tabs on the backs of the legs extend beyond the seam joining the front and back leg pieces, 12 and 15, at the top. Sew these seams on the right side of the fabric, after the leg has been assembled and stuffed. Then insert the tabs between the body front and back at the bottom, and handstitch into place.

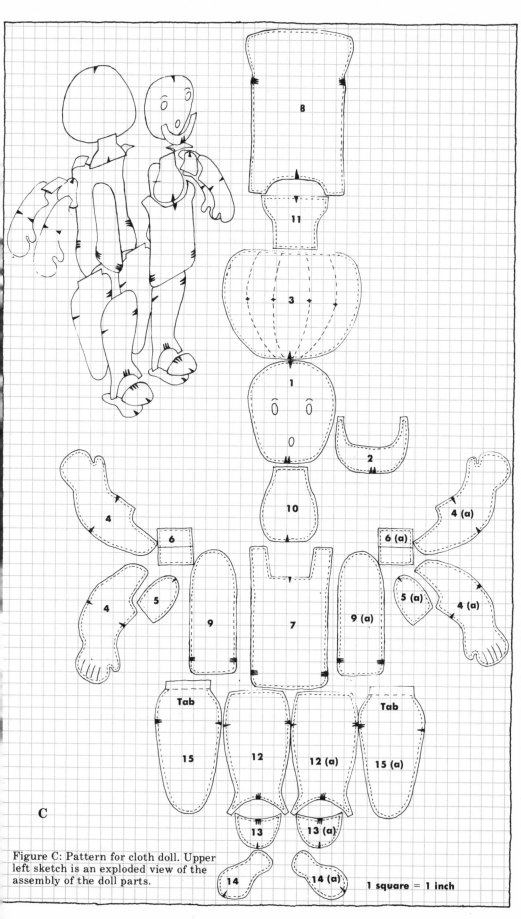

C

Figure C: Pattern for cloth doll. Upper left sketch is an exploded view of the assembly of the doll parts.

1 square = 1 inch

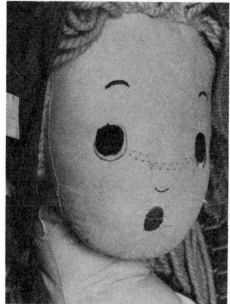

19: Close-up of the doll's face and neck shows use of satin stitch for the mouth and around the black felt pupils of the eyes, the seed stitch making the freckles, the outline stitch making the nose, and the way the finished head section fits down over the doll's neck. The wool strands making up the hair are sewed to the hairline, then pulled straight back from the doll's forehead.

Strings for Folk Songs

Richard Manley teaches woodworking and dulcimer construction at the Craft Students League *in New York City. A graduate engineer and a one-time computer installer and programmer, his love of woodworking and music led him to change careers and establish his own business of building dulcimers and other stringed instruments. He assembles and sells his fine, handcrafted musical instruments in suburban Croton-On-Hudson, New York.*

There is nothing more rewarding than to be able to build something that is both beautiful to look at and beautiful to listen to. Remember the childhood fun of making objects that produced sounds—a musical comb or a willow whistle, for instance? The step beyond that—making something that will produce real music—is an even more satisfactory pastime.

Music is an essential part of everyday life, and this was demonstrated by the first settlers of the Appalachian Mountain region, who sought to make music in the American wilderness as they had in their native countries. There was room only for necessities in the small ships crossing to the new land, so few musical instruments could be brought along. But the settlers did bring memories of the European folk instruments that brightened their lives, and as a result of their attempts to reconstruct these instruments, the Appalachian dulcimer was born.

The word dulcimer is a combination of the Latin *dulce* ("sweet") and the Greek *melos* ("song" or "strain"). A stringed instrument of that name is mentioned in Syrian writings that date from 3000 B.C., but all we know about this instrument is that it was long, narrow, and had three strings. The Appalachian dulcimer at left is a descendant and a consolidation of four European folk instruments—the German *scheitholt*, the French *epinette des Vosges*, the Norwegian *langeleik*, and the Dutch *humle*. All of these were long, narrow stringed instruments that were played held horizontally on the lap or on a table. The first American dulcimers were box-shape, but gradually a violin-like hourglass shape and a teardrop shape (left) became predominant.

The dulcimer is popular today for the same reasons that it caught on when it first was made in America hundreds of years ago: It is easy to play, it is small and transportable, and it provides the right sound to accompany traditional ballads. Dulcimers are sold at relatively low cost in kit or finished form, but if you like working with wood, build your own. It can be any of a number of shapes, of any kind of wood, have whatever shape sound holes you like, and have three, four, or more strings. In other words, it can be personalized in different ways, without any appreciable effect on the sound. The toy dulcimer in the project that follows is a strung fret board without a sound box, yet it sounds as authentic, when played on a carton or table, as a real dulcimer. For this project, the frets, (metal wires against which the playing string is pressed to change a note) are staples driven into the fretboard.

Front view (at the left) and side view (above) of a dulcimer are pictured here to show details of this unusual instrument. Looking at the front view the top is the nut end and the bottom is the bridge end. The string on the far left is the melody string, and the other two are drone strings that are kept at fixed pitches and give the dulcimer's sound its unusual quality. To make this dulcimer, see page 80.

Fretboard dulcimer

Making a toy dulcimer (right) will familiarize you with some of the mechanics of building a real one (page 80), and will give you the opportunity to learn to play a dulcimer without a great investment of time and energy.

Materials and Tools

I used found materials where possible. These include two small pieces of wood ⅛-by-⅜-by-1½ inches for the two string supports (they can be cut from a piece of scrap wood, an old ruler, or a piece of wood molding); three wood screws to anchor the strings at one end; a large cardboard carton, visible in the photograph at right, to act as a sound box; and, to play the dulcimer, a popsicle stick for a noter, and a wedge cut from a plastic food storage container top for a pick. Articles you will need to purchase are: A 30-inch piece of 1-by-2-inch trimmed hardwood lumber; three autoharp or harpsichord tuning pegs; and a set of three dulcimer strings. The dulcimer strings can be purchased at a music shop and so can the tuning pegs, although they may be more difficult to find. If you have difficulty locating any, you can order them by mail from Zuckerman Harpsichords Inc., 160 Avenue of the Americas, New York, N. Y.

Tools you will need are a ruler and pencil, a crosscut handsaw, medium-texture sandpaper, a heavy-duty staple gun and staples, a hammer, a screwdriver, a hand or power drill with a ³/₁₆ bit for drilling wood, and a pair of slip-joint pliers for turning the tuning pegs.

Getting Started

Place the 1-by-2-by-30 inch board on your work table, and with ruler and pencil, mark a line across board width 1⅞ inches from one end and another line 2 inches from the same end. These two lines, ⅛ inches apart, outline the groove that will be cut for one of the string supports. This will be the tuning-peg end, and the string support at this end is called the nut.

With ruler, measure down fretboard from line drawn 2 inches from end, and mark off fret points (photograph 1, and table below). Mark two lines ½ inch and ⅝ inch from tail end of board (opposite tuning-peg end). These lines outline the groove for the bridge (tail-end string support).

Cut the small pieces of wood for bridge and nut. Both should measure ⅛-by-⅜-by-1⅝ inches. Cut three saw-cut wide, diagonal notches for strings into one edge of the top of the nut. Notches should be ⅛-inch deep and cut into outer top edge of nut at about 45 degrees; inner top edge is not notched. Locate one notch at mid-point of the 1⅝-inch length of the nut, and the

Jean Ritchie, born in Viper, Kentucky, is a well-known dulcimer performing artist. Her ancestors, of Scotch-Irish origins, have been filling Kentucky's Cumberland Mountains with the sound of the dulcimer for generations. Now a resident of Long Island, N.Y., Miss Ritchie is the author of Singing Family of the Cumberlands and The Dulcimer Book. Here she plays the children's dulcimer that she designed. The cardboard box performs somewhat the same function as the sound box on a real dulcimer. The sound holes are cut in a traditional heart shape.

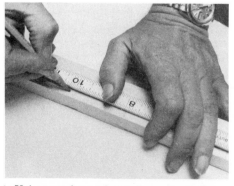

1: Using a ruler and pencil, mark off the fret points near the edge of the board with small lines. Measure from the inside edge of the nut and follow the measurements in the table at the right.

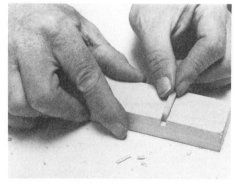

2: Fit the nut into its slot. If you were careful not to make groove wider than ⅛ inch, the nut will fit tightly and require hand pressure to insert all the way. Put bridge in place in the same manner.

FRET MEASUREMENTS:
Distance, in inches, from near edge of nut to center of each fret:

1	3	9	16¾
2	5⅝	10	17¼
3	6⅞	11	18½
4	9⅛	12	19½
5	11¼	13	19⅞
6	12⅛	14	20¾
7	13⅞	15	21½
8	15⅜		

other two ⅜ inch in from either end. The bridge is not notched.

Set bridge and nut aside and go back to fret board. With saw held in horizontal position, cut grooves for nut and bridge. For each groove, first make two saw cuts ³/₁₆-inch deep just inside the two pencil marks. Then saw in between until groove is ⅛-inch wide and ³/₁₆-inch deep. Press nut and bridge into their grooves (photograph 2). If groove is too tight, sand it with sandpaper wrapped around popsicle stick. Glue is not needed if cut is exact.

Insert screws for anchoring strings, and add frets (see photographs 3 and 4). Next, drill holes for the three tuning pegs and insert pegs as shown in photograph 5. To string, tune and play the fret board, see the next to the last paragraph on page 87 and the Craftnotes on page 86.

3: Make pilot holes for screws with a nail, then insert screws with screwdriver. Place screws roughly the same distance from each other as are the string notches in the nut. Let screws protrude ¼ inch.

4: Center a staple on one of each penciled fret mark (see photograph 1, page 79). Position them along board edge nearest you when nut end is at your left. Staples will lie beneath melody string.

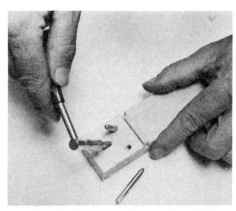

5: After drilling holes for the threaded tuning pegs, screw pegs into the board until they begin to come out the other side. A tuning wrench is being used here, but a pair of pliers will also work.

The outdoors is the dulcimer's concert hall. Miss Ritchie is playing an old teardrop dulcimer. The Ritchie family has preserved and passed on many English ballads (Barbry Ellen, Lord Randal) well-suited to the dulcimer's plaintive sound.

Appalachian dulcimer

To make the teardrop-shape dulcimer pictured on page 78, it helps to have woodworking skill. But a beginner, being very careful about measuring, sawing and fitting, can manage the project if he allows plenty of time for it. Only hand tools are required, and your neighbor may be able to supply you with those you don't have. The tools needed are: A metal ruler calibrated to thirty-secondths of an inch; adjustable T-square; wood vise; plane; saw; five or six C-clamps; jigsaw; fine rasp; rattail file; drill with ⁹/₁₆, ½, ⁷/₃₂ and ¹/₁₆ inch bits; mat knife; thin-blade dovetail saw or fret saw; wire cutters; hammer; protractor; and small paintbrush.

For the dulcimer parts shown opposite, you will need two 32-inch pieces of 1-by-6 and one 16-inch piece of 1-by-4 hardwood lumber; it can be cherry, birch, walnut, mahogany or maple. Other materials needed: A good supply of No. 80 (coarse) and No. 120 (fine) sandpaper; palm-size block of cork; large bottle of white glue; scrap wood for bracing and clamping; ¾-inch thick plywood board 29½ by 8 inches; one sheet of carbon paper and one of tracing paper; masking tape; four 2½-inch finishing (no head) nails; three ⅜-inch roundhead brass nails; thirty ½-inch nails; linseed oil and turpentine. The instrument parts needed are three guitar tuning-gear assemblies with 1¹/₆-inch shafts and screws for fastening (see photograph 29, page 87); two feet (or, if already cut, 17 1¼-inch pieces) of guitar fret wire; and a set of three dulcimer strings. The instrument parts (and the fret saw if you don't have one or a thin-blade dovetail saw) can be purchased at music stores that repair stringed instruments. Or, if you can't find them there, you can order them from a catalog obtainable from H.L. Wild, 510 E. 11th St., New York, N.Y. 10009.

Basic Assembly

In brief, the dulcimer is assembled as follows: The lumber is cut for fret board, front, sides, and back; the front, side and back pieces are split; back pieces are glued together; lumber for neck is cut to size and split; neck pieces are glued together, and cut out; tail block is cut out; sides are shaped and glued to tail and neck; fret board is fastened to front pieces; back and front are glued to sides, and then back and front overhang is cut off along side curves. Follow this detailed procedure:

Cutting Wood for the Fret Board and the Sound Box

The first step is to saw the fret board and the front, side, and back pieces shown in figure A, below. Saw one 32-inch piece of 1-by-6 into two widths, one 3¾-inches wide from which the back pieces will be cut, and the other 1¼-inches wide for the fret board. Saw the second 32-inch piece of 1-by-6 into two widths, one 3¼-inches wide from which the front pieces will be cut, the other 1¾-inches wide from which the sides will be cut. Set the fret-board piece aside for the present. Save excess for cutting nut and bridge.

Now rule a line down the center of the ¾-inch thickness (a purchased 1-by-6 is actually ¾-by-5⅝, of course) of each of the remaining three pieces. Saw through each to split it into two thinner pieces of same length and width (photograph 6). Or have this done where wood is purchased; make sure it is understood wood must be split exactly down middle. You will now have three pairs of wood pieces. Label sawn and unsawn sides and where each piece is to be used. Sawn surfaces will face inside finished dulcimer. Clamp one piece at a time to your work table and plane sawn side to a thickness of ⅛ to 3/16 inch. Always put piece of scrap wood between clamps and good wood. Plane with grain, away from clamp; change clamp to other end and finish operation. Sand planed surfaces with #80 sandpaper wrapped around cork block (cork has just the right consistency to make a good hardwood sanding block). After sanding, always wipe sanded surfaces with a soft dry cloth. Put aside the pieces for the front and the sides.

6: Saw through board's ¾-inch thickness as shown to make thin wood for sound box. Stop periodically to move board up. Put scrap wood between vise and good wood.

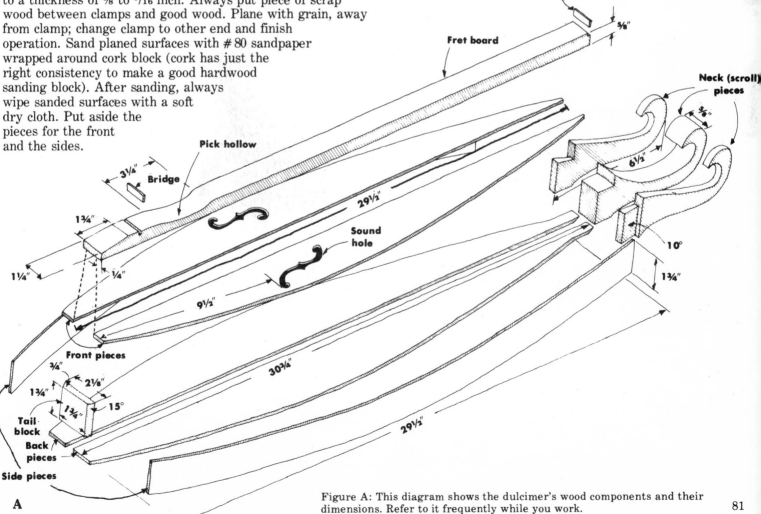

Figure A: This diagram shows the dulcimer's wood components and their dimensions. Refer to it frequently while you work.

Gluing Pieces for the Back

Hold back pieces together so grain patterns on unsawn sides match. Plane edges that will be joined (see figure A, previous page, and photograph 7) until they fit together smoothly. Sand with block and No. 120 paper. Apply glue to both edges and smooth with fingers. Rub boards together to further distribute glue, and with unsawn surfaces up, clamp firmly together. Remove excess glue. If boards don't lie flat, clamp scrap board on top (photograph 9). When glue has set (about one hour), remove boards and sand seam on both sides with cork-block sander—first with No. 80 paper, then No. 120.

Making the Neck

The neck piece (scroll) is a three-piece wood sandwich (see figure B opposite). Cut the 16-inch piece of 1-by-4 into two 6½-inch lengths. Save (for dulcimer's tail block) the 3-inch piece left over. Make outer two neck pieces by splitting one of the 6½-inch pieces into two ⅜-inch-thick pieces. Plane each on sawn sides to 5/16-inch thickness. Sand with cork-block sander and No. 80 paper. The other 6½-inch length is for neck's middle piece. Do not split it, but plane it to a thickness of ⅝ inches. Sand with sander.

With tracing paper, trace all solid and dotted lines, including hole crosses, of neck pattern (figure C, page 84). Then place this tracing-paper pattern, with carbon paper underneath, onto one side of ⅝-inch-thick block. Line up block edges with dotted pattern edges, and retrace dotted line shown in red in pattern (figure C). Lift paper and carbon; line should be on wood.

Place block in vise and cut along carbon line with jigsaw to remove U-shape section of wood. Save it. File and sand cut (photograph 10). To join scroll outer pieces to inner piece, and to finish cutting, follow the directions of photographs 11, 12, and 13. File and sand sawn surfaces as was done on inner piece (photograph 10). Then turn over tracing-paper pattern and, with carbon, transfer the dotted line hole crosses to the other side of the cut-out scroll. Be sure, when doing this, that scroll pattern edges are lined up with actual scroll edges.

To drill the tuning-peg holes, use a 7/32-inch bit. Mark off length of tuning-peg shaft (1 1/16 inches) on your drill bit by wrapping bit with masking tape at a point 1⅛ inches from its tip. Discount cone-shape point of bit when measuring its length. Set neck in vise and push U-shape piece, cut out earlier, back in place between outer pieces of sandwich to prevent wood from splintering. To keep drill from slipping, first lightly hammer a starter hole with a nail where hole center lines cross. Then, stopping when you reach tape edge on bit, drill two holes on one side, turn block over, and drill one hole on other side. Drill will go through one outer piece and slightly penetrate other. Remove U-shape scrap and set neck aside until later.

7: Place back pieces one on top of the other (sawn sides out and grain patterns matching). Plane edges simultaneously. When planing, hold pieces in place with clamped scrap-wood pieces, as shown.

8: Wait five minutes after joining pieces, and remove excess glue with end of scrap-wood stick. Do this every time you glue. Also, put cloth or wax paper underneath so pieces do not stick to work table.

9: Hold boards of back, unsawn sides up, in jig of clamps and scrap wood. If they won't lie flat, clamp scrap piece on top, as shown. Always, before gluing, test by placing the pieces to be glued in clamps and scrap wood to make sure the arrangement works.

10: Smooth jigsaw cut in center block at neck (see text above) with rounded side of a rasp. Smooth cut further with No. 120 sandpaper wrapped around rasp.

11: Glue and clamp three scroll pieces together (see figure B). Align bottom and sides. Let glue set. Remove clamps and file bottom and sides flush.

12: Transfer solid lines and hole crosses of traced pattern (page 84), with carbon, to one side of scroll block. Align dotted line with inside-piece cut.

13: To cut out scroll, saw along solid lines of pattern with a jigsaw, with block clamped. You will have to remove clamp and re-clamp as you saw each section.

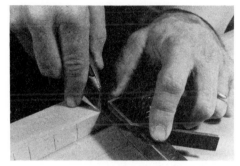

14: Measure from near edge of nut notch, and mark frets (see table, right) on tape stuck to board side. Holding T-square to mark, cut across top with mat knife.

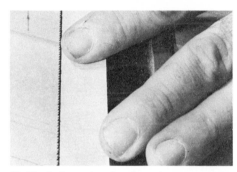

15: Mark fret-wire depth on fret saw with masking tape. Cross-section view of wire is T-shape. Measure depth of ridge that forms T bottom (¹/₁₆-inch) and tape on saw.

16: Align T-square with knife cut, and saw fret notches up to tape on saw. Make sure cut is to full depth of distance marked so wire will sit snugly in groove.

Preparing the Fret Board

Take the 1¼-by-¾-by-32-inch fret board and cut its length to 29½ inches. With No. 80 paper, plane and sand its ¾-inch depth to a depth of ⅝ inches. Use this planed surface as the back of the fret board. Sand sides with No. 120 paper. Rule a pencil line across board width ⅛ inch from one end to mark edge of notch where nut will fit (see figure A, page 81). To measure, mark and cut the 17 fret-wire notches, follow steps in photographs 14 through 16.

After cutting fret notches, rule two lines ⅛-inch apart to mark position of bridge (see measurements, right). Bridge and nut grooves both must be ³/₁₆-inch deep and ⅛-inch wide. Mark ³/₁₆-inch depth with tape on fret saw. For bridge groove, make two ³/₁₆-inch deep cuts at bridge pencil lines, and then make cuts in between until groove is complete. Nut groove is at board end and open on one side (see figure A, page 81); make one cut ³/₁₆-inch deep at pencil line and another at right angles to it ⅛-inch into board end. Sand both grooves with No. 120 paper wrapped around popsicle stick.

Draw a 3¼-inch long indentation, no deeper than ⅜ inch, on fretboard sides for pick hollow (see figure A). File and sand it out.

Finishing the Neck and Making the Tail Piece

Draw two lines on top of neck-piece end at 10-degree angles from corners (use protractor, and see figure D1 on following page and figure A, page 81). Do the same on bottom and saw into neck along these lines. Then cut into both sides of neck, to free the two wedge-shape pieces shown as red areas in figure D1. The dulcimer sides will fit into these triangular recesses.

To make tail block, take the 3-inch piece of 1-by-4 (actually ¾-by-3½) left when originally cutting wood for neck, and cut out a piece measuring 1¾-by-¾-by-2⅛ inches from the middle of its 3½-inch length. Use

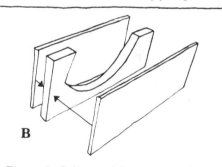

Figure B: Split wood forms outer pieces of neck sandwich. U-shape is cut from the middle piece before gluing.

FRET MEASUREMENTS:
Distance, in inches, from near edge of nut to center of each fret and edges of bridge:

1	2²⁷/₃₂	11	17¹³/₁₆
2	5⁷/₁₆	12	18²⁵/₃₂
3	6²¹/₃₂	13	19¼
4	8²⁷/₃₂	14	20¹/₁₆
5	10²⁵/₃₂	15	20²⁵/₃₂
6	11¹¹/₁₆	16	21⁷/₁₆
7	13¹¹/₃₂	17	21¾
8	14¹³/₁₆	near edge of bridge	26²⁷/₃₂
9	16⅛	far edge of bridge	26³¹/₃₂
10	16²³/₃₂		

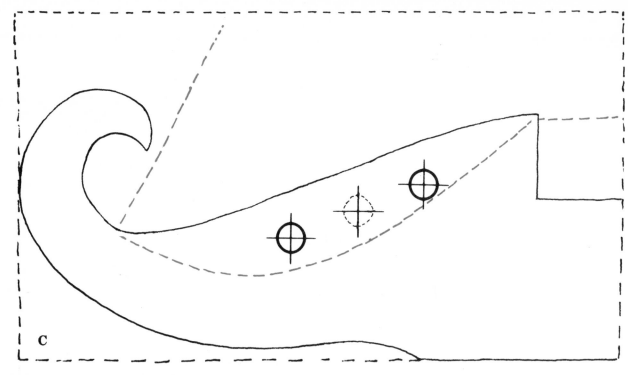

Figure C: Actual-size pattern for scroll and tuning-peg holes. Trace and transfer to wood with carbon.

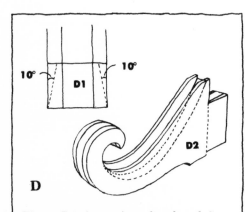

Figure D1: A top view of neck end. Saw along dotted lines. D2: Completed neck piece. Saw into straight dotted line on sides, to free wedge-shaped piece.

leftover end pieces later for clamping. Bevel the tail block according to measurements and angles in figure A, page 81. Then sand the bevels with No. 120 paper.

Use a plywood piece measuring 29½ by 8 inches as a frame on which to shape sides and glue them to neck and tail pieces. Rule a centerline down length of plywood. Center neck, face down (with L-shape notch on neck fitting around edge of board), at one end of line and tail block at other. Clamp both securely (see photograph 17). Rule another line crossing centerline at right angles at a point 12 inches from tail block. On cross line, 3 inches from centerline on each side, hammer a finishing nail to depth of about ½ inch (see photograph 17). Glue and clamp ends of sides to neck (photograph 18). Shape sides around nails and glue and clamp tail block (photograph 19). Leave in place and go on to the next step.

Cutting the Sound Holes and Finishing the Front

Cut both front pieces to 29½-inch lengths. Transfer pattern, figure E, for sound hole onto one of the front boards (see figure A, page 81). Position it

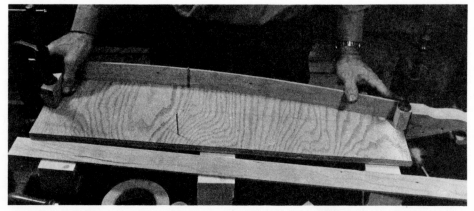

17: Place wax paper or cloth under neck and tail pieces to catch glue, and clamp both to plywood board. Hammer finishing nails, and test position of sides, as shown.

18: Apply glue, and clamp side pieces to neck bevel. Use two pieces of wood cut at 10-degree angles between clamps and sides. Be sure unsawn side surfaces face in.

so larger circular opening is an inch from one edge, smaller is ⅜ inch from other edge, and larger is 9½ inches from tail block end. Align this board on top of other front board, back to back, and clamp to scrap wood to keep them from splintering when drilled. Drill larger sound hole circle with a 9/16-inch bit and smaller with a ½ inch bit. Remove clamps and align the three boards in your vise. Cut out rest of sound hole with jigsaw. To do this, remove one end of saw blade from its frame, insert it through one of the holes, and attach it to frame again. Smooth cut edges with rattail file, and

19: Apply glue to other end of sides, bend around nails, and clamp to tail, as shown. Use pieces sawn off when making tail, as scrap between clamp and sides.

20: Glue front boards to fret board. Before glue sets, hammer ½-inch nails at 2-inch intervals along edges of both front boards. Keep boards aligned at ends.

21: Lightly hammer the pieces of fret wire, toothed-ridge down, into the notches on fret board. Use scrap wood between hammer and wire, to protect wire.

22: When all the fret wires are in place, file both ends with flat side of the rasp until flush with fret-board sides. Then file tips at 45-degree angle to finish.

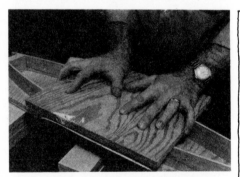

23: For accurate sanding of side edges, use a sanding board made of scrap board and some No. 80 sandpaper. Attach the sandpaper to the board with white glue.

then sand with file wrapped with No. 80 paper. Be careful not to bevel edges.

To attach front boards to fret board, place fret board, back side up, on work table. On both sides of it, place pieces of scrap wood the same thickness as the fret board. Rest the two front boards on these, planed side up, so they are lined up lengthwise at both sides of fret board, and each overlaps the fret board ¼ inch. Make sure pick hollow of fret board and larger circles of sound holes on front boards are both closer to the tail end, and that smaller sound-hole circles are the ones closest to the fret board (see figure A, page 81). Glue and nail front boards to fret board (see photograph 20). When glue has set, turn over front assembly, sand fret-board top, and round edges slightly with block sander and No. 120 paper. File and sand a slight incline on 1¾ inches of fret-board tail end (see photograph 26, page 86).

Fastening the Back and the Front to the Sides
Unlike any of the previous steps in the assembly of the dulcimer, the two steps of gluing the back and then gluing the front to the sides must be done on the same day to avoid warping. First, place one or two 6-inch lengths of scrap wood at points where they will fit snugly between the two sides still

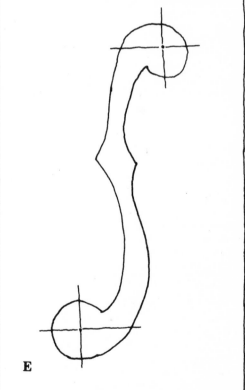

E

Figure E: Trace this pattern, including hole crosses, and transfer to wood with carbon.

DULCIMER CRAFTNOTES

Tuning and Playing the Dulcimer.
By turning the tuning pegs, tune the first and second strings to G above middle C and the third string to middle C, itself. You can use a piano or pitch pipe, but if you have neither of these, tune your dulcimer by ear. Tighten the third string until it is under a fair amount of tension. With your left-hand thumb, press the string onto the fret board to the left of the fourth fret (count from the tuning peg end placed at your left). Pluck the string with your right hand. The pitch you hear is what the first and second strings should be tuned to.

The proper way of playing the dulcimer is to sit on a fairly low stool or chair, and rest the instrument on your lap with the scroll to your left (see photograph 30, opposite). The noter (a 3 to 4-inch length of narrow bamboo cut from a garden stake or a popsicle stick) is used to change the pitch of the melody string only. Hold it between the thumb and forefinger of your left hand and rest the end of it on the first string, with the side of your forefinger against the side of the fret board. This will enable you to slide the noter up and down the melody string without touching the second string.

With the noter, press the melody string to the left of the third fret. Pluck the string with your right hand; the note you hear is C. To play the scale of C Major, pluck the melody string, as you slide the noter up to each successive fret, stopping at the tenth (press the strings just to the left of each fret for the best sound). Do this again, but instead of plucking the melody string only, strum all the strings with a pick in your right hand, while sliding the noter to each fret, as above.

For an ideal pick, cut a rounded triangle out of the top of a plastic food storage container. You can use a guitar pick, but they're a bit too stiff for smooth dulcimer playing.

A turkey or goose quill is the traditional pick (see photograph of Miss Ritchie, page 80).

Play the scale up and down until you feel comfortable with the instrument, and then try to pick out some simple tunes. For further information about tuning, and for some music to play, see *The Dulcimer Book* by Jean Ritchie, Oak Publications, 33 W. 60th St., New York, N.Y. 10023.

24: After applying glue to the side pieces and the back piece, clamp them in place, as shown. Clamp the neck and tail ends first and then clamp the sides.

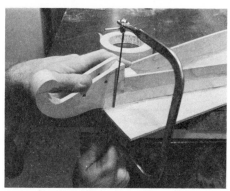

25: Saw off the back-piece overhang as close to the sides as possible without touching. Also saw off overhang of the side pieces at the tail end, and front piece, when attached. Sand small remaining overhang flush with sides.

26: Hammer the nails that will secure the strings into the incline on the tail end of fret board. Place in any pattern, as long as each lines up along fret board with one of the notches in the nut. They should protrude 3/16 inch.

clamped to frame (see photograph 24). Fashion a sanding board to sand side edges (see photograph 23, previous page). Remove clamps from one end to sand it, replace and then remove from other end. Do not remove nails from frame.

Take the assembled piece for dulcimer back and saw it to a length of 30¾ inches. Lift dulcimer side, ends, and rib supports in one piece off nails and frame. Place back board, planed side up, onto some scrap wood supports and rest dulcimer assembly scroll up, on top of it (see photograph 24). Center it and align tail piece with one end and beginning of curve on neck bottom with other end. As a guide for gluing, trace around side edges. Replace in position, clamp until glue sets, then saw as in photograph 25. Clamp and sand top edges of side pieces with sanding board as before. Glue front assembly to sides in same manner that back was glued (see above), with the exception that front is glued *down* onto sides. Clamp and let glue set. Remove clamps, saw off overhang, and then plane back and front edges. Sand them flush with sides with sanding block and No. 80 paper, then sand all over sound box with No. 120 paper to smooth surfaces and round edges slightly.

Applying Finish
Dulcimers traditionally are not finished as painstakingly as other stringed instruments are. Boiled linseed oil is all that is needed to preserve the wood and give it a rich patina. Brush on a mixture of half turpentine and half linseed oil for first application. Soak 30 minutes and wipe dry. Additional coats of straight boiled linseed oil may be applied until desired sheen is reached. Wait 24 hours between coats, wiping dry 30 minutes after each coat has been applied.

27: For checking height of bridge, string distance above second fret should be thickness of match cover. If distance is too great or small, adjust bridge.

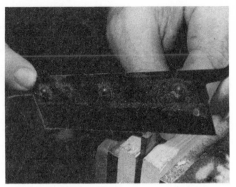

28: Saw shallow angled cuts into one edge of nut with the fret saw. Strings then will touch only a tiny area of the nut. This will assure accuracy of pitch.

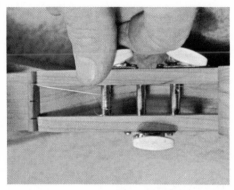

29: Wind each string around one of tuning shafts, as shown. Two pegs of one orientation lie in holes on one side, and one of opposite is in hole on other side.

Stringing the Dulcimer

Put the three tuning pegs in their proper holes in scroll (photograph 29). Mark places for their screws by tapping nail into screw holes while pegs are in place. Remove pegs and drill shallow holes with 1/16-inch bit to start screws. Replace pegs and fasten screws. I used brass nails for anchoring strings at the tail end of fret board (photograph 26 opposite) but any kind of small nail will do. To prevent splitting, start nails by drilling shallow holes with 1/16-inch bit, and then hammer in place.

Cut nut and bridge from leftover wood, and file both to 1¼-by-⅛-by-⅜-inch dimensions. Leave top of nut flat, but round top of bridge. Place bridge in its groove. No glue should be needed for either fret or bridge. They will fit tightly without it. Bridge should protrude about 3/16 inch above fret board, but check its height with one of the strings. Place string loop around one of the nails at tail-piece end, and extend it over bridge and along fret board up to first fret. Press it on first fret and check string clearance on second fret with unfolded match-book cover (photograph 27). If string is too high, file bridge. If too low, make bridge groove shallower with wood filler or put masking tape on bridge bottom. Keep string in place for testing nut.

With fret saw, cut three shallow angled slots in nut (photograph 28). Two outside slots should be ¼ inch in from nut's ends, and middle slot should be ⅜ inch away, on each side, from other slots. Put nut in place so higher sides of angled slots face away from scroll. Strings should touch this side of nut only. To determine proper depth of angled slots, take string still in place and extend it through one of nut slots. Rest it in slot and hold it, without pulling down on it. Make sure string clears first fret by at least the thickness of match-book cover. It is better to have string too high than too low above fret. But try to bring it as close to match-cover thickness as possible. Cut slot in nut deeper, as needed. Make sure angle of cut is great enough so that, when string is in place, it still rests only on side of nut away from scroll. Test other nut slots with remaining strings in same manner.

To string the dulcimer, lay it horizontally in front of you with the scroll to your left. The two thin wire strings of your set should be strung nearest you and the heavier string farthest away. This is the opposite of guitar-string placement. Loop each string on one of the nails at the tail end, and thread it through either of the holes in one of the tuning shafts at the other end (photograph 29). Turn tuning-peg handle so string wraps around shaft. Catch loose end in string being wound. Continue until string is taut. Cut off excess string with wire clippers. For tuning and playing, see the Craftnotes on the opposite page.

30: Mr. Manly shows the correct way of playing. Your dulcimer will provide hours of enjoyment if you learn to play. It's as easy as playing piano with one finger.

Designs That Celebrate Nature

The folk artist, wherever he lives, adopts the animals, flowers, and other natural objects around him as the inspiration for his decorative motifs. His imagination may create strange looking animals, people or plants you have never seen. Still, you can appreciate the way these figures, worked into vivid designs, often became powerful symbols of faith or superstition.

The projects on the following pages provide examples of diverse, but in some ways parallel, folk art in different lands. You can decorate documents and furniture with unicorns, distelfinks (thistlebirds or finches), tulips and other motifs that fascinated German immigrants who settled in Pennsylvania in the eighteenth and early nineteenth centuries. The motifs they used are shown here and on pages 90 and 91. You can also make the mobile weather vane silhouette featuring sprightly reindeer described on page 94. Laplanders used similar designs on weather vanes, barns, and other buildings. Finally, you can create your own folk art, adapting some of the familiar motifs on pages 92 and 93. Just as the Colonists improvised materials and methods, and invented designs, feel free to let your own imagination wander. The keys to folk art are boldness, individuality, and simplicity of expression.

Barbara Auran-Wrenn designs craft kits, and lectures and writes on contemporary crafts. As an indication of her wide-ranging interests, Barbara describes the decoration of native objects by Pennsylvania Germans and a variety of international folk art symbols.

Making a fraktur traufscheine ¢ ▨ ♣ 🦃

During the eighteenth and nineteenth centuries, Germans emigrating to Pennsylvania (commonly called the Pennsylvania Dutch, after the word *Deutsch* meaning German) to escape religious persecution brought with them a highly developed folk art. One example of it was *fraktur schriften* (meaning broken writing, so called because of the sharp, angular lettering used). This was a blend of folk designs with Germanic script, as shown at left. *Fraktur schriften,* or *fraktur* as it was more commonly called, was adapted from the quill-lettered script and brush-painted designs of medieval German illuminated church manuscripts. By the middle of the eighteenth century, *fraktur*-style decorations were being applied to personal documents, furniture, glass, pottery, linens and even buildings.

A favorite candidate for *fraktur* art was the marriage certificate or *traufscheine* (from *trauf* meaning marriage and *scheine*, meaning certificate). These certificates were often decorated with an expanded heart flanked by the wedding couple as shown opposite. To make such a *traufscheine*, trace the patterns shown opposite, or develop your own design, using motifs shown on pages 92 and 93. You won't need the goose quill pen, plant pigment inks and rag paper used by the original *fraktur* folk artists. But you will need 8½-by-10-inch sheets of tracing paper and carbon paper; a piece of 12½-by-15-inch mat illustration board; a ruler; pencil; gum eraser; stylus; black ink; masking tape; No. 1 and No. 3 sable brushes; paper towels; and tempera paints for your design. I used yellow ochre, olive, rust, sky blue, orange, black and white. Local art supply stores stock the matboard, brushes, stylus and paint.

Lightly tape the tracing paper over the illustration opposite, so it won't shift as you draw. Copy the outline of the heart, the figures, tulip, and arch. Then lightly mark horizontal guidelines for the written inscription. Lift the tracing paper off. With a ruler and pencil rule a border two inches in from the top and sides of the illustration board and three inches in from the bottom. Lay the carbon paper within the border of the illustration board and center the tracing over it; tape both down. With a dull hard pencil or stylus, impress the pattern onto the surface of the board. Using the illustration opposite as your color guide, paint the designs. With a stylus dipped in black ink or a black ball-point pen, write in script the couple's names, and the date. Use gum eraser to remove pencil marks and the certificate is complete.

German colonists in the U.S. often commissioned artists to design birth certificates or *taufscheine* (from *tauf* meaning baptism, and *scheine*, meaning certificate) for their newborn. This *taufscheine* was lettered and painted in *fraktur*, a style named after the sharp, angular lettering used. (The German word *fraktur* means to break or fracture.) Inscribed on the certificate are the child's name, birthdate and a brief family history.

A

Figure A: The bride and groom, expanded heart and tulip shown here were popular *traufscheine* motifs.
Other motifs commonly found were trumpeting angels, shooting stars, and doves.

Figure B: Unicorns shown paired and rampant were a favorite dower chest motif. Occasionally they were shown singly, with a lion or horse opposite them. Unicorns were supposed to be drawings of rhinoceroses artists had heard about but never seen.

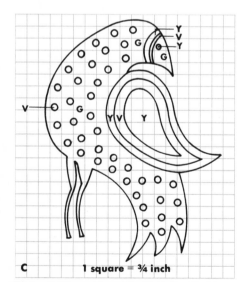

Figure C: The position of the bird's head is characteristic of the distelfink or goldfinch design used by the Pennsylvania Germans on their wares. Other popular bird motifs included doves, eagles, pelicans (as symbols of maternal devotion), and paired robins (as lovebirds). Color key to paint enlarged distelfink is Y, chrome yellow, V, vermillion and G, olive green.

Figure D: Tulips and unicorns (the traditional guardians of maidenhood) were popular motifs on dower chests. The owner's first name was often lettered free-hand in a blank bar below a hex sign. Hex signs were geometric designs intended to attract good luck (in this case, make the sun shine), or to ward off such trouble as demons and lightning.

Decorating a hope chest

A *fraktur* marriage certificate or *traufscheine,* as used by the Pennsylvania Germans, was traditionally pasted inside the lid of a dower chest. This was a hope chest designed to serve both romantic and practical functions. When a young girl reached marriageable age, she stored linens and laces inside the chest. After marriage, in a couple's sparsely furnished dwelling, the chest doubled as a seat by day and a child's bed at night. It also served as a trunk when goods had to be transported. The bride's father or the decorator who designed her marriage certificate applied appropriate motifs to the chest. These symmetrical designs were scratched into the wood's surface with a metal stylus or painted freehand. Some typical designs for such a chest are shown on these two pages. The front of the chest opposite consists of three evenly spaced arched panels. Sometimes additional single panels were applied to each end of the chest. On more elaborate chests the front middle panel bore the bride's first name as on the unicorn panel opposite, and sometimes the date and year of presentation. Inscriptions were often bordered by tulips, hearts, and unicorns (the traditional guardians of maidenhood).

Undecorated dower chests can sometimes be found at country sales or in antique shops. Furniture stores stock unfinished storage chests which approximate the 22-by-28-by-48-inch size of the chest in the color photograph below. To paint the background and feet of such a chest, you will need one quart of primer and about two quarts of oil base paint. Raw umber paint was used for the background color of the chest below, but barn red, dark green and dark blue are also traditional colors. You will need to mix a pint of white and ½ tube of raw umber paint to paint the background of each panel ivory. Limit yourself to five colors for ornamentation so your design doesn't become too busy. Oil-base yellow ochre, Prussian blue, vermilion, chrome yellow, and olive green are suggested colors. To thin paint and clean brushes you will need 12 ounces of turpentine. Other essentials are: a 2-inch nylon paint brush; a No. 4 sable brush for designs; masking tape; ruler; compass; 3 sheets of 14-by-20-inch carbon transfer paper (dressmaker type); 3 sheets of 14-by-20-inch tracing paper; plenty of rags and newspapers. Place the chest in a large, well-ventilated space that can enable you to work on several sections of the chest simultaneously and decrease drying time of painted surfaces.

Spread newspapers over your work area. If you are working with raw wood, seal the surface of the wooden chest with a coat of primer. To use the unicorn/tulip design (Figure B) for your center panel and the small tulip design (Figure E) for your side panels, trace the designs on tracing paper and enlarge them as indicated following instructions on page 158. Lay the chest on its back and tape the enlarged tracing of each panel with a piece of carbon underneath it to the chest front. Leave 2½-inch spaces at the sides and between each panel. The midpoint of the top rounded arches on each panel should be located four inches below the chest lid. Trace only the outlines of each panel. Remove tracing. Cover background of chest outside the panel areas with two coats of raw umber paint and fill each panel with two coats of ivory. Allow two days for the paint to dry between coats.

Retape tracings on top of carbon transfer papers to chest so that panel outlines match. Then transfer outlines for designs within panels. Use illustrations (Figure D and Figure F) for color guides as you paint in the design details.

To decorate the ends of the chest, enlarge the distelfink design (Figure C) by tracing it on a grid according to instructions on page 158. Transfer the design to the ends of the chest as you did the front panels. Center each design five inches from either edge of the chest, with the top of the bird's head four inches below the top lid. To paint the bird, use vermilion, olive green and chrome yellow oil-base paint, as indicated in Figure C.

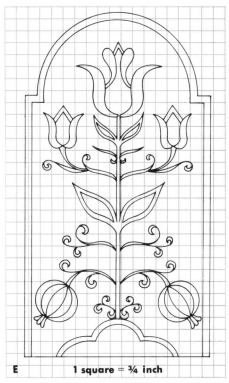

Figure E: Tulips symbolized the Trinity. This design, enlarged to scale shown, can be used for two smaller panels flanking a unicorn center panel on your dower chest.

1 square = ¾ inch

Figure F: Follow this color scheme to paint tulip panels after tracing design on chest.

Tulips growing out of slender urns were painted on each arched panel to decorate this antique eighteenth century Pennsylvania German dower chest. Vines and leaves tie together the design. You can decorate a similar chest using the unicorn panel (opposite) and the tulip panel (right).

Native Decorations

In many lands magic and fertility cults developed which were accompanied by folk decorations. Today, most of these cults have disappeared, but we can still enjoy the expression of these early myths through native designs.

G

Figure G: The tulip is a familiar folk art motif throughout Central Europe and in America. When used in groups of three, it was originally thought to represent the Holy Trinity.

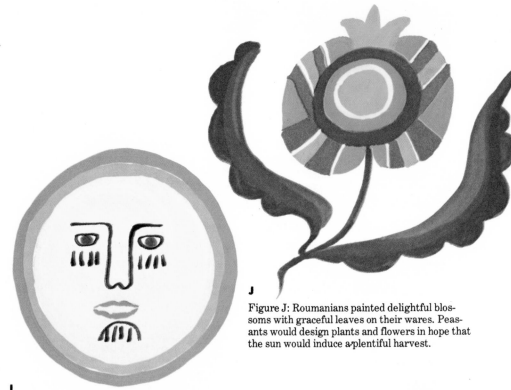

I

Figure I: Roumanian folk artists gave the round sun human facial qualities. It symbolized life, energy and a good harvest, and was a widely used decoration on linens and clothing.

J

Figure J: Roumanians painted delightful blossoms with graceful leaves on their wares. Peasants would design plants and flowers in hope that the sun would induce a plentiful harvest.

H

Figure H: Flowers like this were commonly embroidered on Ukranian linens. Flowers were associated with curative powers, the promotion of good health, and the encouragement of sunshine.

K

Figure K: The silhouette of this rooster was cut from paper and decorated with colored paper shapes. Poles associated the rooster with fertility and hung these bird designs in their homes.

Figure L: This water buffalo design is a tribal motif taken from an appliqued umbrella. African kings gave umbrellas decorated with such motifs to brave warriors.

Figure O: This bird, which was sewn on a towel, has a golden crown that suggests power. It is a Ukranian motif believed to attract good fortune and repel evil forces.

Figure N: This version of a folk art heart is believed to have originated in Russia. Folk artists from many lands use heart motifs as a symbol of fertility, good crops and love.

Figure M: Spotted reindeer detail was hand-painted on a Roumanian plate. The designs that accompany the reindeer on the dish recount the story of a famous hunt.

Figure P: This is a Kurbits, a large flower drawn by Swedish folk artists as a symbol of the flower thought to have protected Jonah from the sun as he wandered through the desert.

Reindeer weather vane

The folk sculpture pictured below is an adaptation of a Lapland reindeer design. It can be hung indoors as a wall plaque, or mounted outdoors as a weather vane, as Laplanders mounted theirs atop barns, churches, houses and ships. The decorative weather vanes had to be clearly silhouetted against the sky, so they could be read quickly from a distance. Carved motifs included animals, heraldic designs, biblical figures or trade symbols reflecting the special interests of local craftsmen.

To make the reindeer decoration shown below, you will need a 4-by-36-inch and a 10-by-36-inch piece of 1-inch-thick pine, poplar or maple; a 6-inch length of ⅜-inch doweling; a set square; a calibrated T-square; 4 sheets of medium-fine sandpaper; a vise, two 3-inch C-clamps; cheesecloths; 4 ounces of white glue; two 1½-inch nails; two ½-inch-long screw eyes; a hand jigsaw or sabre saw with a woodcutting blade; a drill with ⅜-inch and ½-inch diameter bit at least 6 inches long. From art supply stores, you will need: 1 pint each of barn red and slate blue acrylic paint, and 2-ounce tubes of yellow ochre, black, and white acrylic; a No. 2 sable brush, a 1-inch bristle brush; 4-by-36- and 10-by-36-inch sheets of tracing paper (you may have to tape several smaller sheets together); 8-by-10-inch sheets of carbon paper; 4 ounces rubber cement and a rubber cement pickup; 3 feet of picture wire.

If you want the reindeer to be a weather vane, you will need: a ½-by-48-inch rustproof metal rod and a sturdy wooden or metal base with a center hole ½ inch in diameter to balance and support the entire structure (hardware or naval supply stores and mail order catalogs for farm equipment carry a selection of manufactured weather vane bases); and 2 pieces of ½-inch-by-6-inch scrap metal for the metal strips to make the bent tail decorations in the photograph shown below.

Clamp the two 36-inch-long boards so their ends are flush. Measure 18 inches in from one end and use the T-square to mark a vertical centerline through both boards. Then, following the instructions on page 158, carefully enlarge the patterns in Figure T, opposite, and transfer them onto tracing paper. Coat one side of the 4-by-36-inch and the 10-by-36-inch pieces of wood and the backs of the base and reindeer tracings with rubber cement. Allow the cement to dry thoroughly. Then, using the centerline marked on the boards as a guide, gently press the 4-by-36-inch tracing for the base and the 10-by-36-inch tracing for the reindeer over the corresponding pieces of wood.

Clamp pieces of wood in a vise and cut along pattern outlines with a jigsaw or sabre saw with a wood-cutting blade. When both patterns have been cut out and rough edges sanded, line up the centerlines and peg marks you had previously

George Cohen was born in St. John, New Brunswick on the Bay of Fundy. He moved to New York City in 1925 and worked as a fabric and furniture designer. Now retired, he has begun a new career as a sculptor. He works mainly with wood scraps that he collects, assembles, carves and paints. His designs add a touch of humor and sophistication to old-world folk art themes.

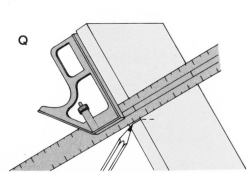

Figure Q: Use a set square to transfer drilling marks (dashed lines on pattern, figure T) to the bottoms of the legs and the top of the base.

The carved sculpture above was adapted from a Lapland folk motif. Cut-out areas enhance the profile of the simple design, which can be hung on a wall or mounted as a weather vane.

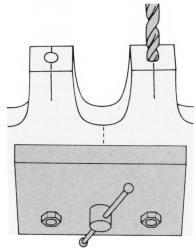

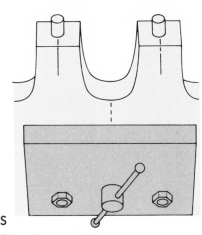

Figure R: Drill ⅜-inch-diameter holes ¾-inch deep for the four pegs to be placed in each fore and hind leg of the reindeer decoration. Drill four corresponding holes in the base.

Figure S: Apply white glue to the tip of each peg and insert into fore and hind legs of the reindeer decoration. These pegs will fit into holes on the base when you are ready to assemble.

marked on both. Lift off tracing and use rubber cement pickup to remove excess cement. Adjust tracings over cut wood pieces to center circle atop triangle and zigzag designs on reindeer front. Lay carbon paper beneath designs on tracings and use a pencil to transfer designs onto wood surface. Then transfer drilling marks for the location of dowel holes from the side to the edge of each board as in Figure Q. Divide thickness of board in half and mark center for drilling.

Drill four ⅜-inch-diameter holes to a depth of ¾ inch at the marked centers in the reindeer legs and base (Figure R). If you are making a weather vane or plan to add curved metal tails as shown in the color photograph opposite, drill a ½-inch-diameter hole through the center of the reindeer and the base. Smooth all rough edges with medium-fine sandpaper.

Cut the ⅜-inch dowel into four 1½-inch lengths. Cover one end of each peg with white glue, then insert one in each of the four legs (Figure S). After cleaning areas to be painted with rubber cement pickup, coat the front and edges of the reindeer with barn red acrylic paint thinned to creamy consistency with water. For an antique finish, streak the painted surface by dragging a cheesecloth across it while the paint is still wet, following the same direction as the wood grain. Allow paint to dry for one hour, then repeat the process on the reverse side. Next coat one side of the base and edges with thinned slate blue paint and streak the surface with a cheesecloth. When the paint has dried, repeat the procedure on the back. Dip a corner of a cheesecloth into thinned black paint and speckle the front and back of the reindeer and base by dabbing cloth against the wood; allow 30 minutes drying time. With undiluted black, yellow ochre, and white acrylics, fill in the details on the reindeer and base with a No. 2 sable brush. Use the color photograph opposite as your painting guide. Apply white glue to the protruding pegs in the reindeer legs and push them into the corresponding holes in the base. Wipe off excess glue. Shape the ½-inch strips of scrap metal to make the curved tail decorations shown in the color photograph. Push them into the top of the hole drilled through the center rump that both reindeer share. To complete the weather vane insert a ½-by-48-inch metal rod through the bottom hole of the base and reindeer. Place the rod within a wooden or metal weather vane base that has a corresponding ½-inch hole long enough to balance the weight of the weather vane. Secure the stand in an unsheltered spot on your deck, roof, or in your garden where the weather vane will be visible from a distance and can revolve freely.

To use the reindeer design as a wall plaque, simply twist two small screw eyes into the middle of the back of the reindeer, spacing them about 13 inches apart. Run a 15-inch length of picture wire through the screw eyes and twist 2 inches of each end of wire around itself, snug at the eye, to secure. Suspend the sculpture from two nails spaced 12 inches apart.

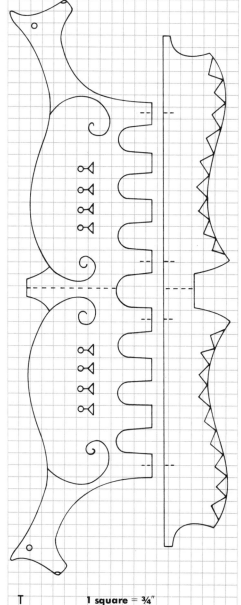

T   1 square = ¾"

Figure T: When enlarging and tracing the patterns for the reindeer and its base, be sure that you transfer all design lines and dotted guidelines for the pegs that hold the two parts together.

HOME BREWING
With Roots and Herbs

Nicholas E. Leddo has been making wines and beers, alcoholic and nonalcoholic, for 15 years. He has conducted a television series on winemaking and has lectured extensively on brewing.

From Colonial times until quite recently, the brewing of soft drinks and ales was a popular domestic art in America. Of the two types of brew, beer was the more important to the Colonists. In fact, it was a factor in the *Mayflower's* landing at Plymouth instead of Virginia. A 1622 manuscript records the decision made during the historic voyage of 1620: "for we could not now take time for further search or consideration, our victuals being spent, especially our beer." The first commercial brewery in America was built a year later in lower Manhattan by the Dutch West India Company.

Early commercial breweries were like the one shown on this page, where horses, plodding around a capstan in the brewery basement (see inset at right) provided the motive force for grinding grain, usually barley, which makes the malt used in beer recipes. A series of cogwheels (F and G) powered by the capstan in the basement turns the grindstone (H). Grain arrives from the

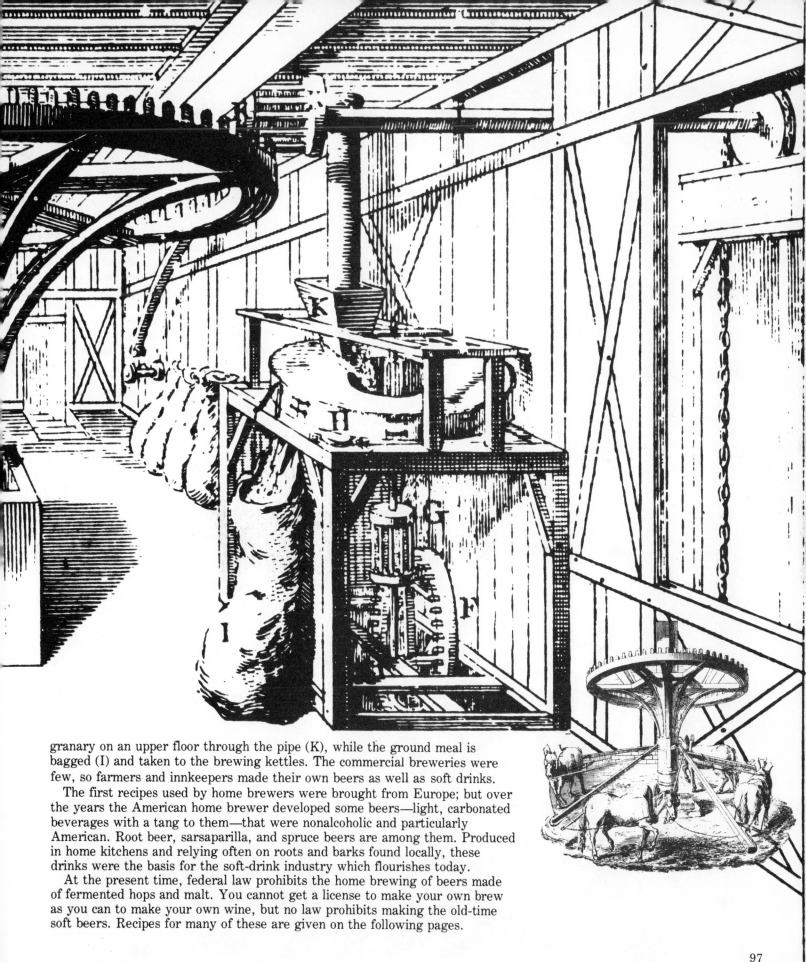

granary on an upper floor through the pipe (K), while the ground meal is bagged (I) and taken to the brewing kettles. The commercial breweries were few, so farmers and innkeepers made their own beers as well as soft drinks.

The first recipes used by home brewers were brought from Europe; but over the years the American home brewer developed some beers—light, carbonated beverages with a tang to them—that were nonalcoholic and particularly American. Root beer, sarsaparilla, and spruce beers are among them. Produced in home kitchens and relying often on roots and barks found locally, these drinks were the basis for the soft-drink industry which flourishes today.

At the present time, federal law prohibits the home brewing of beers made of fermented hops and malt. You cannot get a license to make your own brew as you can to make your own wine, but no law prohibits making the old-time soft beers. Recipes for many of these are given on the following pages.

1: Equipment useful in making soft drinks includes 10-gallon plastic pail; 5-gallon carboy; 5-foot siphon hose; wooden spoon; 2-ounce packet of chlorine detergent; nylon straining bag. To bottle carbonated beverages you will need: bottle filler; bottle capper; crown bottle caps and 12-ounce bottles.

Root beer and sarsaparilla

The beverages below are generally known as soft drinks, but they are not the carbonated drinks you buy ready-bottled at the grocery store. They are naturally fermented brews carbonated by the action of yeast and sugar or other fizzmaking ingredients, such as cream of tartar. They contain a small amount of alcohol, usually less than one-half of one percent, and may be brewed legally without purchase of a license.

Much of the equipment used for making these drinks you may already have in your kitchen, especially if you make your own jams and jellies and have five-gallon kettles for the purpose. The equipment used for making carbonated drinks appears in photograph 1. Indispensable items for carbonated beverages are the bottles made specifically for carbonated beverages, bottle filler, bottle capper and crown bottle caps.

Caution: Bottle carbonated brews only in new bottles purchased for the purpose. Throw-away bottles that have held carbonated beverages from the store may not be strong enough to withstand the gas pressure that builds up in some homemade brews and could burst.

On these pages there are old-fashioned recipes for beverages that are not carbonated and therefore do not require a bottle capper. Try those first to see if making soft drinks and brews is an activity your family enjoys.

Equipment that you can't find locally can usually be purchased from firms that sell brewing supplies, such as Specialty Products International,

Root beer is a favorite soft drink of young and old alike. This brew, homemade, has more body and flavor than commercial drinks.

Ltd., Box 784, Chapel Hill, N.C. 27514, and Wine Art Shop, 1109 Front Street, Uniondale, N.Y. 11553.

Before you make your own brew, sterilize the equipment to be used, the containers, the tubes, and the bottles—even if they are new. The easiest way to sterilize is to wash everything thoroughly with a chlorinated-detergent solution. If the local hardware shops don't carry chlorine detergent suitable for this purpose, buy from a brewing-supply house. Mix two ounces of the detergent with one gallon of warm water, and wash everything in this solution. Be sure to rinse away all traces of the chlorine after the detergent has been used. Any solution left in the bottles or on the equipment might affect brews that include yeast and could spoil the flavor of others.

Root Beer

Homemade root beer is flavored with an extract made from the root of the sarsaparilla plant, a trailing tropical vine, of the *Smilax* genus, that grows in America. The recipe below is typical of soft-drink recipes of home brews.

Root Beer

4 pounds granulated sugar	½ teaspoon dry baker's yeast
4¾ gallons lukewarm water	1 cup lukewarm water
3 ounces root-beer extract	

Place the sugar in a 10-gallon plastic pail, and pour in the root-beer extract. Mix well, to distribute the extract as evenly as possible through the sugar granules. Mix the yeast in the cup of lukewarm water, and let it stand

2: Pour the root-beer extract from the bottle right onto the sugar. Mix thoroughly so the extract is distributed evenly through the sugar.

3: Making the yeast mixture. Sprinkle over the cup of warm water; stir, and let stand. Be sure to use the exact amount of yeast specified in the recipe.

4: Adding water to sugar-and-extract mixture. Pour the water slowly to avoid splashing. Pouring and mixing are easy in a 10-gallon plastic pail.

for 5 minutes. (Do not use more yeast than the recipe specifies; if you do, the drink will be unpalatable and excessive gas pressure may develop in the bottles.) Pour 4¾ gallons of lukewarm water from the tap into the pail to dissolve the sugar. (If stronger flavor is desired, reduce the sugar to 3½ pounds and the water to 4 gallons.) Add the yeast mixture to the sugar mixture (see photograph 5), and blend well. The next step is to siphon the beer into a 5-gallon carboy. Let the mixture rest for an hour so that any sediment (which might affect the beer's flavor) will settle. Then, using the siphon hose or a bottle filler, fill 12-ounce carbonated-beverage bottles to within ½ inch of the top; more air space might cause spoilage. Seal the bottles with a hand capping machine and crown bottle caps (photograph 7).

Keep the bottles on their sides in a warm place away from drafts until you see bubbles forming. Root beer should be ready to drink about 5 days after bottling (longer in cool weather). After 5 days, place a bottle in the refrigerator; chill well, and taste the root beer. If the carbonation is adequate, put the other bottles in a cool place with an even temperature. Just before serving, refrigerate for a short time to make the root beer really cold and to prevent excess foaming. When home-brewed beer is served, fill the glasses or the pitcher in one pouring to avoid stirring up sediment.

Makes about 5 gallons, or about 50 (12-ounce) bottles.

Figure A: During the siphoning process, the exit end of the hose is held high so the beer will be aerated as it splashes into the carboy. Carboy is placed well below the pail so that all liquid is siphoned off, leaving behind as much sediment as possible.

5: Adding the yeast mixture to the sugar mixture. Empty the cup. Then, to make sure all the yeast is added, dip up a cupful of the sugar mixture, swirl it around the cup and dump back into pail.

6: Bottle filler, attached to siphon at other end, is inserted. Lower filler tip to within ½ inch of bottle bottom. You can fill bottles with the siphon end alone, but a filler makes the job easier.

7: Using a hand-operated crown capper. Place the bottle on a block, if necessary, to get it high enough to receive the cap at maximum pressure. Center each cap before pressing down the capping lever.

Other Sarsaparilla Drinks

Commercial root beer is made from a liquid extract of sarsaparilla combined with wintergreen and other flavoring agents. Sarsaparillas were very popular in the late nineteenth and early twentieth centuries, when it was generally believed that sarsaparilla was a tonic and could cure a long list of ailments. So fervent was the belief in its curative powers that many elixirs touted by traveling salesmen were flavored with it, and almost every homemaker had a recipe for making her own sarsaparilla brew. Today, faith in sarsaparilla's medicinal value has vanished, but it still is used to mask the flavor of unpleasant medicines, and it still makes a pleasant, light drink similar to those made in homes long ago.

Compare the modern recipes for Sarsaparilla and Sarsaparilla Syrup below with the recipe for Sarsaparilla Mead, which is more than 100 years old. It appears in a recipe book titled *The Young Homemaker's Friend*, which was written by a Mrs. Cornelius and was published in Boston in 1859 by Brown, Taggard and Chase. Mead is a name usually applied to drinks in which honey is the main sweetener, but the term is also used for many light drinks flavored with sugar rather than honey.

Old-time Sarsaparilla Mead

"Three pounds of sugar, three ounces of tartaric acid, one ounce of cream of tartar, one of flour, one of essence of sarsaparilla, and 3 quarts of water. Strain and bottle it, then let it stand ten days before using it."

The modern version relies on sugar and yeast to start its bubbles going and omits the cream of tartar, tartaric acid, and flour. Although a nylon strainer is called for in the recipe, a clean nylon stocking will do the job as well. Sterilize your equipment as described above, and bottle the drink in 12-ounce bottles intended for carbonated beverages.

Sarsaparilla

9 cups sugar
5 gallons lukewarm water
2 ounces sarsaparilla extract

½ teaspoon dry baker's yeast
1 cup lukewarm water

Dissolve sugar in the 5 gallons of lukewarm water in a 6- or 10-gallon container. Add sarsaparilla extract, and stir thoroughly. Mix the yeast in the cup of lukewarm water until dissolved. Strain through a nylon strainer into the sugar mixture, and stir well. Transfer into sterilized bottles, using the bottle filler or the siphon, as described in the recipe for Root Beer, page 99. Store in a warm place for 5 days. Chill before serving.

Makes 5 gallons, or about 50 12-ounce bottles.

Sarsaparilla made this way is naturally fermented and refreshingly fizzy. You can also make an excellent sarsaparilla drink with Sarsaparilla Syrup, below. Just mix the syrup with sparkling club soda.

Sarsaparilla Syrup

7 cups sugar
4½ cups hot water

2 ounces sarsaparilla extract

Pour the sugar into the hot water in a 3-quart kettle or a plastic container. Add extract, and mix well. As soon as the sugar is completely dissolved, the syrup is ready to use. To flavor an 8-ounce glass of club soda, add 2 or 3 tablespoons of syrup. Makes enough to flavor 40 to 50 8-ounce drinks.

Sarsaparilla is only one of the many root and bark flavorings used to make soft drinks. The early recipes given on pages 102 to 105 are similar to the modern versions that follow them. Some of the ingredients in the early versions—pine buds, for instance—are hard to find, but many of them can be purchased from herb stores and mail-order supply houses such as Caswell-Massey Co. Ltd., 320 West 13th Street, New York, N.Y. 10014.

Reproduction of an old soft-drink poster advertising root beer in the early days of commercial soft drinks, when many people on homesteads and farms were still brewing their own cooling potions.

Ginger beer, other delights ¢ 🔲 🚹 🔬

Another old-time favorite is ginger beer, translated by the soft-drink industry into ginger ale. It is interesting to compare the three following recipes. The Nineteenth-Century English Ginger Beer uses brown sugar and lemons, with ginger and cream of tartar and yeast for flavor and fizz. The two modern recipes rely on ginger and yeast, but resemble the 1859 version.

In preparing the brews in this section, follow the same general procedures described for Root Beer, page 99. The equipment is essentially the same—hose and bottle filler for siphoning (to avoid transferring sediment to bottles), large plastic pail for the mixing. The bottle capper, bottles, and crown caps will be needed for beverages that will be carbonated. Sterilize the equipment before using it, as instructed on page 99.

Drinks that have yeast as an ingredient generally taste better if they are allowed to rest several days before they are served, so the flavor can ripen and the sediment settle. Those without yeast usually can be served at once. In these recipes, as in those with sarsaparilla root, the water is lukewarm to dissolve the sugar easily. But if you are planning to mix the ingredients in a crock or a large, heavy container instead of a plastic pail, it is a good idea to warm the crock or container first by scalding it with a kettleful of boiling water, as suggested in the recipe for Yankee Switchel, page 104.

Nineteenth-Century English Ginger Beer

"Pour four quarts of boiling water, upon an ounce and a half of ginger, an ounce of cream of tartar, a pound of clean brown sugar, and two fresh lemons sliced thin. It should be wrought twenty-four hours, with two gills (½ pint) of good yeast, and then bottled. It improves by keeping several weeks, unless the weather is hot, and it is an excellent beverage. If made with loaf instead of brown sugar, the appearance and flavor are finer."

Modern Ginger Beer I

2 cups sugar
2 lemons
6 quarts warm water
¼ teaspoon dry baker's yeast

1 cup warm water
1 tablespoon cream of tartar
2 tablespoons ground ginger

Mix sugar and juice of the lemons in a large bowl. Pour in 6 quarts warm water, and stir well to dissolve sugar. Let stand until tepid. While mixture is cooling, dissolve yeast in 1 cup warm water, and add to cream of tartar and ginger. Add this to sugar mixture, and stir thoroughly. Pour into 12-ounce bottles for carbonated beverages, and seal with crown caps. Lay bottles on their sides in a cool place 5 days. Beer is then ready to serve. Makes 16 (12-ounce) bottles.

Modern Ginger Beer II

1 ounce fresh ginger root
1 pound loaf sugar
½ ounce cream of tartar
2 lemons

1 gallon rapidly boiling water
½ ounce yeast cake
2 teaspoons granulated sugar

In a small mortar or on a wooden cutting board, bruise the ginger root. Put it in a 4-quart bowl or kettle with loaf sugar and cream of tartar. With a potato peeler, peel rind from lemon as thinly as possible. Remove white pith with a sharp knife. Slice lemon thinly. Add lemon peel and slices to ginger mixture. Pour boiling water into the bowl; stir with a wooden spoon. Let

The popularity of brewing in medieval times is reflected in this period woodcut of a reveler with a glass of beer.

Homemade ginger beer occasionally develops quite a head and has a sharp, tangy flavor. It is flavored with either fresh or ground ginger.

cool to lukewarm. Cream yeast with granulated sugar, and add to the mixture. Cover bowl with foil, and leave it for a day in a moderately warm room. Then strain liquid through a nylon strainer. Bottle and cap as in preceding recipe. Let rest 4 days. Chill before serving.

Makes 10 (12-ounce) bottles.

A variation of ginger beer is Switchel, an old-time Yankee thirst quencher.

Yankee Switchel

2 gallons warm water
4 cups sugar
2 cups molasses

2 cups good cider vinegar
2 teaspoons ground ginger

Scald a 4-gallon crock or kettle with a kettleful of boiling water. Pour in the warm water. Stir in sugar and molasses, mixing until sugar has completely dissolved. Stir in vinegar and ginger, and mix well. Let cool. Bottle in 2 sterilized gallon jugs. Store in refrigerator.

Makes 2 gallons.

Other Types of Root-Flavored Beer

The recipe for Nineteenth-Century Spring Beer, the most complex of the three early recipes given below, calls for wintergreen, pine buds, molasses, yeast, and hops. The recipe for Spruce and Boneset Beer also relies on hops for flavor. Boneset, *Eupatorium perfoliatum*, is a North American herb once believed to be helpful in the setting of bones.

Nineteenth Century Spring Beer

"Take a handful of checkerberry (wintergreen), a few sassafras roots cut up, a half handful of pine-buds, while they are small and gummy, and a small handful of hops. (If dried in the ordinary way. But a small pinch of hops put up in pound packages by the Shakers is enough.) Put all these into a pail of water over night, and in the morning boil them two or three hours; fill up the kettle when it boils away. Strain it into a jar or firkin (¼ barrel) that will hold half a pailful more of water. Stir in a pint and a half of molasses, then add the half pailful of water, and taste it. If not sweet enough add more molasses. It loses the sweetness a little in the process of fermentation, and should therefore be made rather too sweet at first. Add two or three gills (½ or ¾ pint) of good yeast, set it in a warm place, and let it remain undisturbed till it is fermented. When the top is covered with a thick, dark foam, take it off; have ready clean bottles and good corks; pour off the beer into another vessel, so gently as not to disturb the sediment; then bottle it, and set it in a cool place. It will be ready for use in two days. The sediment should be put into a bottle by itself, loosely corked, and kept to ferment the next brewing."

A current recipe for Modern Spring Beer follows much the same procedure and is made with similar ingredients.

Modern Spring Beer

4 pounds brown sugar
2 cups dark molasses
3 quarts boiling water
1 ounce essence of sassafras

4 ounces cream of tartar
1 ounce essence of checkerberry (wintergreen)

In a 1-gallon crock or kettle, mix sugar, molasses, and boiling water. Use the last bit of boiling water to rinse out the cup in which you measured the molasses. Stir until water becomes lukewarm. Then add cream of tartar. When cool, add checkerberry and sassafras; mix well. Store in a 1-gallon jug, capped, in the refrigerator. Use 2 tablespoons of this mixture to 8 ounces of cold water. To make a fizzy drink add ⅓ teaspoon baking soda to each glass.

Makes enough for about 150 (8-ounce) glasses.

Modern Spruce Beer

2 quarts of boiling water
½ teaspoon oil of spruce
½ teaspoon oil of sassafras
½ teaspoon oil of wintergreen

2 gallons cold water
1½ pints dark molasses
1 cake yeast, crumbled

Pour the boiling water into a 5- or 10-gallon container. Stir in spruce, sassafras, and wintergreen; mix well. Stir in the cold water, molasses, and yeast. When yeast is completely dissolved, siphon mixture into a carboy; let rest 2 hours. Then bottle in 12-ounce bottles; cap. Let settle 48 hours before serving. Serve well chilled.

Makes 26 (12-ounce) bottles.

The following nineteenth-century recipe for various beers, from spruce to boneset, is similar, and is from Mrs. Cornelius' *Advice to Young Homemakers*.

Early Recipe for Spruce and Boneset Beer

"Boil a small handful each of hops and boneset for an hour or two, in a pailful of water; strain it, and dilute it with cold water till it is of the right strength. Add a small tablespoon of essence of spruce, sweeten, ferment and bottle it, like spring beer.

"The essence of hops, checkerberry, ginger, and spruce, put into warm water in suitable proportions, then sweetened, fermented, and bottled, make good beer."

Spruce, with its tart, gummy taste, was an ingredient in many cooling drinks. There is no well-known modern equivalent for the Maple Beer recipe below, but once you have made some of the soft drinks described here, you may want to try your powers of interpretation on this set of ingredients. The unusual combination promises an interesting drink.

Brewer, circa 1600.

Early Recipe for Maple Beer

"To four gallons of boiling water, add one quart of maple syrup and a small tablespoon of essence of spruce. When it is milk warm, add a pint of yeast; and when fermented bottle it. In three days it is fit for use."

Kvass

Kvass, or quass, enjoys a traditional popularity among the peoples of Russia and eastern Europe. It is made by fermenting yeast and stale bread (usually rye) with the addition of sugar and sometimes fruit. With the following recipe, you can produce a drink with an exotic taste. The flavor of kvass isn't quite like that of any other drink.

Kvass

2 pounds dark rye bread
8 quarts water
3 tablespoons dry baker's yeast,
  or 3 cakes yeast

1 quart warm water
⅔ cup honey
3 or 4 sprigs fresh mint

Slice bread thinly, and bake slices in oven at low temperature until they are crisp. Bring 8 quarts water to a boil in a large pot. Place rye rusks in the water, and let them soak 3 to 4 hours. Then strain liquid into another large pot. Dissolve yeast in 1 quart warm water. Add this to liquid from bread mixture. Then add honey. Crush mint, add, and stir thoroughly.

Place cheesecloth over the pot, anchoring it with string or tape. Put pot in a warm part of the room, and let the mixture ferment 6 hours. When froth appears, strain the kvass, and funnel it into 12-ounce size carbonated beverage bottles. Use the capper to seal with crown caps. Store in a cool place and let rest 6 days. Chill for several hours before serving.

Makes 21 (12-ounce) bottles.

INDIAN CRAFTS
Beadwork and Moccasins

American Indians, regardless of tribe, have a rich art and craft heritage that is second to none in the variety and complexity of its skills. It would take several volumes just to catalog the ancient and modern uses to which these skills have been and are being put.

There are, however, two American Indian handicrafts that are especially popular today: Indian beading and leatherwork. Try to think of a shoe store that doesn't stock moccasin-style footwear. And think of all the beaded headbands, belts, and other Indian-inspired fashion accessories sold all over the world.

To learn to duplicate the authentic Indian-crafted objects of the past would present a unique challenge to ingenuity and intellect. But by following the instructions that begin on the next page, you can make an almost limitless variety of authentic Indian and Indian-inspired beaded accessories—from diamond-shaped rings to daisy-chain necklaces and bracelets—in the designs suggested or in designs you create yourself. You also can make your own moccasins—in both low-top and high-top styles—as the Apache Indians have been making them for hundreds of years.

Alvina Mofsie and her daughter Josephine Tarrant are Indian artisans well-known for their skill in beadwork, which is the craft specialty of their tribe. Born in Nebraska on a Winnebago Reservation, Mrs. Mofsie has lived in New York since 1929. Mrs. Tarrant lives in New Jersey.

Origins of Indian Designs

Designs for authentic Indian motifs for beadwork can be divided into two types, determined by the natural surroundings familiar to the artisans. Woods Indians were the traditional creators of patterns based on flowers, leaves, trees, and animals. When fluid, curved lines appear in Indian work, these also usually can be attributed to tribes from wooded areas. In contrast, the Plains Indians of the American Southwest were inspired by the straight-lined geometric forms of their environment—the flat-topped mesa, for example, and the great desert expanses.

Compared to the leather crafts, beadwork is a relatively new Indian craft, although Indians have been making bead ornaments from shells, bones, seeds, pods, and other natural materials since the earliest times. Beads were also a medium of exchange. Wampum belts, made of beads cut from seashells, had designs that recorded events in the history of the tribe and were used for bartering. But the execution of designs with glass beads began only after the arrival of Europeans, who first brought glass beads to this hemisphere at the time of Columbus. The Europeans traded the beads for the Indians' more valuable furs. In working with glass beads, the Indians translated the traditional designs originally executed by artisans using porcupine quills. This accounts for the straight, geometric lines of much modern beadwork.

Material

Generally, the materials you will need—beads, wire, beeswax, needles, and thread—to make the projects that follow can be purchased at a well-stocked hobby or crafts shop. If there isn't such a shop near you, you should be able to find most, if not all, of the required supplies at the crafts, trimming, notions, stationery counters of any large department store, or even those of five-and-dime stores. Loom beading, of course, requires a simple loom, available at craft shops. Instructions for making one inexpensively yourself are given on page 111.

Beaded medallion, about four inches in diameter, was traditionally worn as an ornament on a headband, a bandolier, or on ceremonial clothes. Project directions are on page 110.

Brilliantly colored geometric motifs of these beaded pieces are typical designs of the American Plains Indians. Work such as this is generally made on a loom and then sewed to fabric or leather.

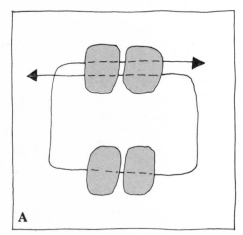

Figure A: First step in making a ring.

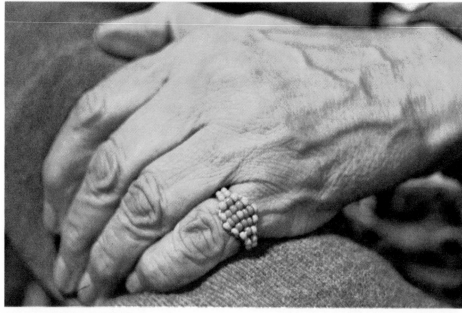

The hands that made and model this ring are those of our Winnebago Indian artisan Alvina Mofsie. The same technique also can be used to make bracelets and necklaces.

1: String a blue bead, an orange bead, and another blue bead on the right-hand wire. Pass the left-hand wire through all three beads; then pull both wires slowly in opposite directions. Take care not to kink wires when pulling.

2: String a blue bead, three orange beads, and another blue bead on the right-hand wire. Pass the left-hand wire through all five beads, and pull both wires until the new row is neatly set against the three-bead row below.

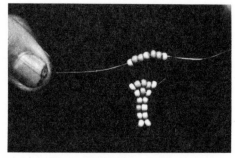

3: String a blue bead, two orange beads, another blue bead, two more orange beads, and a last blue bead on the right-hand wire. Put the left-hand wire through all seven beads, and pull. At this point, the ring is more than half completed.

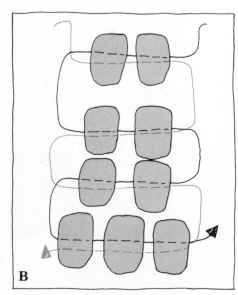

B

Figure B: Finishing a beaded ring.

Beaded ring

Although Indians generally did not wear beaded rings, the designs used for bracelets, headbands, and bandoliers do make attractive rings.

Making the Ring

□ Cut an 18-inch length of No. 30 stainless-steel wire, and string two blue beads to its center. See figure A.

□ Then string two blue beads on the right-hand wire. Pass the left-hand wire through both beads, and pull wires slowly—wire kinks easily—in opposite directions. See figure A.

□ Continue stringing two blue beads at a time until the chain, placed under your ring finger, reaches the sides of your finger.

□ Follow the instructions given with photographs 1, 2, and 3 above. Then repeat the steps described for photographs 2 and 1, in that order.

□ Now all you have to do is join the ends of the diamond-shape ring by passing the wires through the beads as shown in figure B.

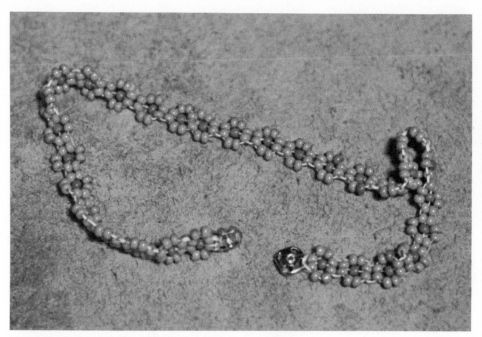

Necklace made with the daisy as a motif uses a design taken from nature, one which often appears in the work of contemporary American Indian artisans.

Mass-produced seed beads are often uneven in size and shape. Mrs. Mofsie takes great care to select only uniform beads for her daisy chain.

Beaded daisy chain

The daisy is a traditional Indian motif which here is incorporated in a chain. Once you have grasped the basic technique you can adapt it to make necklaces, bracelets, and earrings. Daisy ornaments also can be appliqued to fabric or leather.

Instructions for Making Daisy Chain

□ Draw thread hard across block of beeswax, and thread the needle. Double the thread over, and knot the ends together.
□ String eight blue beads, and go back through first bead. See figure C1, which illustrates the process.
□ Add an orange bead, and go through bead A. See figure C2.
□ Add blue beads C, D, and go back through beads B, A, C, D. See figure C3.
□ Add six blue beads, and go through bead C. See figure C4.
□ Repeat steps 3, 4, and 5 until daisy chain is of desired length.
□ Sew ends together, or add snaps or hook and eye.

The orange center bead (see also figure C2 below) matches in size and harmonizes with the surrounding blue beads of the daisy-chain petals.

▼ Figure C: The four steps used in making the daisy chain.

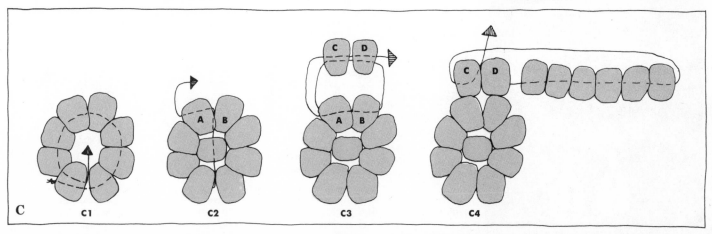

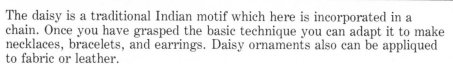

C   C1   C2   C3   C4

Medallion

To make a medallion, you need bead graph paper, two No. 10 needles, No. 50 mercerized-cotton thread, beeswax, a No. 110 needle, thin, stiff cardboard, and two pieces of felt slightly larger than your medallion.

On graph paper, plot your own design or that of the medallion on page 106. Thread the needle; double the thread; knot; beeswax. Follow figure D.

Next, string and lay out the first plotted ring. Then, as shown in figure E, pass the needle back through A, B, and send it down next to B. Bring the needle back up half a bead width from B, ready for stringing the second ring. Thread the second needle; double thread; knot; beeswax. Send it up between center bead and D, E. Then send it down to tack, D, E. Repeat at F, G, so that all beads are tacked in groups of two (A and B are already secured). Tack all succeeding rings the same way.

After following the instructions for photographs 4 through 7, you will have a medallion to hang from, or stitch to, anything you would like to decorate.

▲ Young Kevin Tarrant wears headband and necklace ornamented with medallions.

▼ Medallion incorporating daisy motif is decorated with shells.

Figure D: Glue cardboard to back of square of felt and sew bead through the center.

Figure E: Use both beading and tacking needles to secure rings, as shown above.

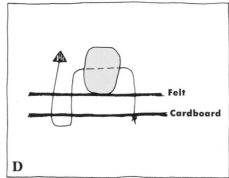

4: Each ring must be closely inspected for design conformity before it is tacked down. Seed beads too large or too small can destroy the symmetry of the design.

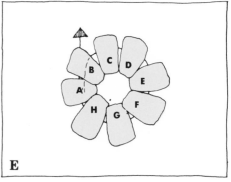

5: When medallion design is completed, carefully trim excess felt and cardboard, without cutting any stitches. Then cut another felt circle for final backing.

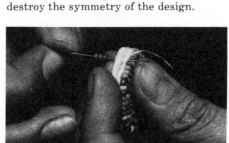

6: The second felt backing is sewed on with a finishing stitch that makes a gay border around the medallion. String three beads, and send the needle from rear to front.

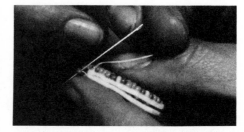

7: Catch the front bead (the last bead strung), and pull until the center bead stands straight up. Repeat, using two beads, until border has been completed.

Loom beading

8: Four pieces of scrap wood and eight nails are materials needed to make loom.

9: To string loom, tie No. 8 cotton thread around sidepiece end.

10: After winding as many strings as you will use, tie thread again to sidepiece.

11: With your fingers, gently space warp threads a bead width's distance apart.

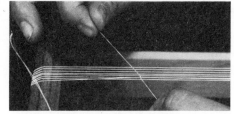

12: Thread No. 12 needle with No. 50 cotton thread. Double; tie to outer warp.

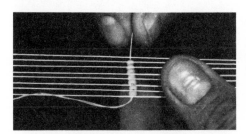

13: String beads, and position them underneath and between the warp threads.

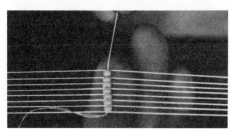

14: Gently push beads up above the warp threads, and pass needle through them.

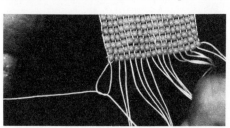

15: Tying ends is easy with an even number of warp threads. Just pair them, and knot.

16: To finish the piece, tape ends, and fold them under where they won't be seen.

Many American Indian beadwork pieces are made on a loom, which allows the artisan to work with several strands of beading at once. A beading loom is simply a rectangle consisting of four pieces of wood nailed together.

The loom used to illustrate the looming technique of beading, photograph 8, was made from 18-by-1½-by-½-inch and 6-by-3-by-¾-inch pieces of wood. You can use wood of any length and width as long as the finished loom is sturdy, level, and longer and wider than the beadwork you wish to create. Make sure that the side-pieces are low enough to allow you to reach over them to work under the warp threads strung lengthwise on the loom.

Loom-beaded works can be belts, necklaces, headbands, even cat collars. They can be sewed on shirts, dresses, jeans, and jackets, or they can stand on their own merits without any material backing.

Work with a Graph

For your first loom-beading project, copy any of the American Indian designs shown in this article, or make up one of your own. Once you have decided on a design, the best thing to do is to work it out in color on bead graph paper, or you can use ordinary graph paper, which usually is available where school supplies are sold. After your design has been put on graph paper—one square for each bead—you will have a bead-by-bead color guide for each row to be loomed.

To loom, follow these procedures:

Use beeswax on the weft (crosswise) thread that goes through the needle.

Use an odd number of beads for the rows. This will allow you to use a center bead in your design.

Be sure you have strung one more warp (lengthwise) thread than the number of beads needed in each row.

Knot weft thread to warp thread several inches up on the warp, to keep warp thread ends long enough to be tied off later.

Pull weft thread firmly, but gently. Pulling too tightly would make the edges of your work uneven.

Instructions for loomwork are given with photographs 9 to 16.

Apache moccasins

When man first came to the North American continent, he probably was wearing some sort of leather footwear. In the time between that migration and the advent of white men, the original footwear patterns were adapted to divergent climates and terrains encountered by the Indian nations. Anthropologists believe that the Apache was one of the last Indian tribes to migrate south into what is now the United States, so it is not surprising that some of their high-topped-moccasin patterns resemble Eskimo mukluks—soft boots of sealskin or reindeer skin—and other northern footwear.

I have chosen to describe the making of the low-top, or short-style, Apache moccasin for the following reasons: The soft leather this style requires is easier for the novice to work with than is heavy leather; I have found this moccasin well suited to general wear; and I like its appearance better than that of the high-top variety.

For those who would like a higher moccasin, however, I have described a simple modification of this low style (see page 117).

Some Tips for the Beginner

Three pieces are required for this Apache moccasin: Sole, vamp, and back.

I have found that the most effective way to fit a moccasin perfectly is to make the pieces in that sequence, that is, to make the pattern for a piece only after the preceding piece has been completed. In this way, the pieces are fitted to each other, rather than being cut out all together before being assembled. I measure the vamp piece on my foot without first creating a separate pattern for it. After you have made your first pair, you may develop your own techniques.

When laying out patterns on leather, check both sides of the hide carefully, to be sure you are not including scratches, holes, or thin spots. Try to lay out two corresponding pieces—both soles, for example— side by side in the same direction on the hide. This ensures uniform stretch. Do not cut on the bias (that is, with the pattern laid so that the line from heel and toe runs on the diagonal of the hide—see Craftnote).

Most important: Try on the moccasin frequently as you are making it. Fittings help you understand how to proceed.

Tools

Besides the leather (see Craftnotes, page 116), you need only a few tools and supplies to make the moccasins shown here.

Marking implements: Felt-tip and ballpoint pens; pencils.

Needles: Straight, sturdy needles, 2 ½ inches or longer. Sewing centers sell hand-stitching needles.

Hand-stitching thread: Stout nylon or waxed linen. It can be bought at shoe-repair and leather shops or in the leather district of a big city.

Awl or fid: Used to make holes through which needle and thread run. It must be very thin and needle-sharp at the tip. I use a carpenter's awl.

Cutting tools: A matte knife, or a replaceable block knife, and a wooden board to cut on are used by many professional leatherworkers. Good, sharp scissors are needed to cut leather. Don't use cheap scissors.

Measuring tools: A tape measure and a straight-edged ruler.

Brown wrapping paper: For patterns.

Old leather glove: To protect your hand as you tighten stitches.

Pliers: To pull the needle through tight spots. Usually, if you can't pull the needle through by hand, the awl hole isn't large enough.

Stephen LePage, Vietnam veteran and former supervisor for a leathercraft factory, lives in Shoreham, Vt., with his wife, Lassie. The LePages grow organic vegetables, raise organic beef, make their own footwear, and work at living off the land.

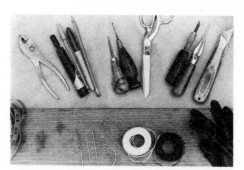

17: Tools: Pliers; felt-tip pen; ballpoint pen, and pencils; carpenter's awl or a fid, used to enlarge holes; scissors; knife of replaceable-blade type; tape measure; brown paper; wooden board; needles; nylon thread; waxed linen thread; leather glove to protect hands when you are pulling the thread through the holes made by the awl.

The design of these leather moccasins made in the style of the Apache Indian originated with the Eskimo. Apaches migrated to the Southwest from Canada about 1200 A.D.

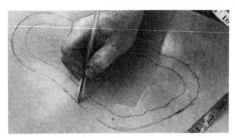

18: Add a ¾-inch margin to the original tracing of the outline of your foot, as shown here. Lean your full weight on your foot when you trace its outline.

19: As you cut the pattern for the moccasin sole, work close to the inside edge of the outer tracing line. Make the cut edge of the leather close to vertical.

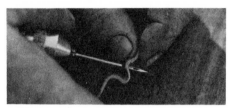

20: With the awl, enlarge each hole for puckering thread. Make holes ⅛ inch apart and ⅛ inch from edge of the sole.

▶ Figure **F**: The sole. Line A-B is midway.

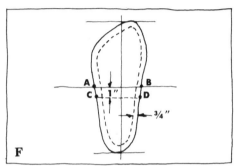

Making the Sole

Start by tracing the outline of your foot on a piece of brown wrapping paper. Keep the pen vertical, to get an accurate outline. Add a ¾-inch margin to the foot outline (see figure **F**), and cut out the pattern. Trace it on the sole leather and then cut the sole out, following this outline.

To shape the leather to your foot, it is necessary to thread a drawstring around the perimeter of the sole piece and draw the edge up about your foot, so that the leather puckers. Holes for the drawstring should be ¼ inch apart and ¼ inch from the edge of the sole. Mark the holes with the point of the awl, then press the awl through the holes. Enlarge each hole with the awl until the needle slides through easily.

Use a four-foot length of thread for the puckering process. Thread the drawstring through the holes, starting at point A and finishing at point A in figure **F**. To pucker the leather, pull hard on the thread. Wet the leather slightly after it has been threaded, to help mold it to your foot. Use a damp sponge, and do not soak the sole, just moisten it.

Shape the sole around your foot. It should fit your foot without binding your toes. The height of the sides of the sole should be equal all around. Tie threads together on the inside, leaving the ends uncut.

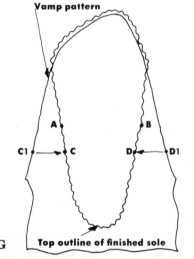

Figure **G**: Untrimmed vamp laid out flat.

21: As you sew, stop every two inches, and pull hard on the thread, to pucker sole edge. Start stitching at point A in figure **F**, and finish at point A.

22: Puckered sole is fitted to your foot after thread has been laced completely around edge. Wet the leather with a damp sponge, to help mold it to your foot.

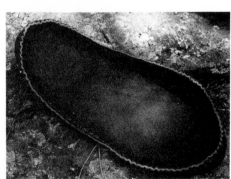

23: Notice here that the thread is tightly drawn at the points of maximum curvature, which shows the most pucker. Thread is only slightly drawn along the sides.

Making the Moccasin Top (Vamp)

On the sole piece, determine points shown as A, B, C, D, in figure **G**. Make a light pen mark at each. Points C, D, are about one inch back from A, B. From your vamp material (see Craftnotes, page 116), cut a piece as long as your foot and twice as wide. Put your foot down on the puckered sole. Lay vamp leather over the foot, and press vamp leather hard against sole edge, to make an impression. Turn the vamp piece over, and trace the sole's impression with your pen. Figure **G** is a sketch of vamp leather with points A, B, C, D, inked in to correspond to sole markings. Draw lines on the vamp piece at right angle to C, D, extending to vamp-piece edges, and draw lines from outer edges of toes to meet these lines at C1 and D1. Cut out the vamp.

24: A piece of vamp material the length of your foot and twice its width is pressed against puckered sole firmly enough to mark the vamp leather.

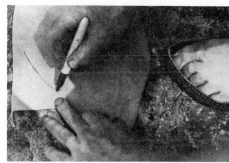

25: Ink the outline made on the vamp underside from tips of toes back to points C, D on figure **G**. It will be clear if you press firmly.

26: With sole and vamp lined up at A, B, C, D, make reference marks on edge of each. This will help you keep pieces lined up when you sew them together.

27: Photograph shows a row of tight, even stitches, and this is your objective: careful sewing that gives a professional look to the finished moccasins.

Attaching and Trimming the Vamp

When you have cut out the vamp, it should resemble figure **G**. Check for fit by laying it on your foot. When you pull up the sole edges to meet the vamp, you should have a tight fit across the ball of your foot and a bit of slack around arch and instep, at C, D. Trim vamp if it is too large.

With sole and vamp on your foot, make ink marks along the cut edges of both at several points, so you can keep pieces lined up as you sew. Thread a four-foot length, and use the whipstitch, figure **H**. Begin at toe. At the first stitch, pull through half the thread; the rest is reserved for the other half of the seam. Pull stitches tight; wear glove, to protect your hand. When you get to point C, or D, tie off the thread, as shown in figure **I**. Thread needle with reserved thread, and sew other side. Tie off.

Put on the moccasin, smooth the vamp, and mark and trim it, as in figure **J**. When fitting the vamp, let it lie smoothly against your instep; don't pull it to either side. When finished, vamp should taper smoothly from C to a width of about three inches at the top. Mistakes in trimming aren't crucial, since the cuts will be covered by the flaps of the back piece.

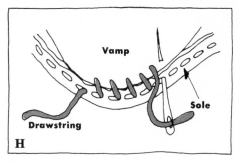

Figure **H**: Whip stitch used to bind sole and vamp pieces. As you work, enlarge every other drawstring hole in the sole, and punch holes in the vamp above sole hole.

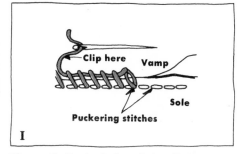

Figure **I**: Backstitch and tie off all threads on the inside of the moccasin: tying off process is essential if the moccasin is to be long-lasting and sturdy.

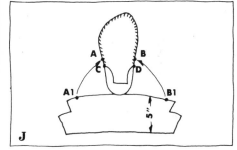

Figure **J**. Back piece of the moccasin. Note that it is slightly curved to fit your heel more closely at the top. Distance A1, B1 equals distance AB measured around heel.

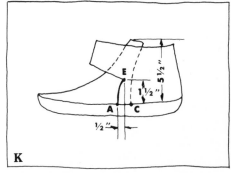

Figure **K**: Sidecuts A, E, (and B, F on the other side of the moccasin) are made after the back piece has been attached to the moccasin.

LEATHER CRAFTNOTES

The following leathers are listed in the order of their availability and are recommended for making moccasins:

Cowhide: After initial tanning, cowhide is 1/4-inch thick and fairly stiff. The tanneries then split it into the desired weights of top grain and suede splits (suede on both sides). The standard unit of leather thickness is the ounce. One ounce equals 1/64 inch. After being split, leather is processed for color, flexibility and surface texture.

Vesting Leather: These moccasin tops are made of vesting leather.

Soft Bag Leather: Similar to vesting leather, but twice as heavy.

Latigo and Other Oil-tanned Leathers: I use it for all my moccasin soles. Light, strong, and moisture-resistant.

Horsehide: Excellent texture and strength, but can be hard to find.

Elk and Moose Hide: Indian materials. If available in correct weight, use it.

Leather Suppliers

Good leather is expensive, but no more so than good fabric. Cowhide costs between fifty cents and one dollar a square foot at this writing—15 to 30 square feet per half hide. Few suppliers will cut up a half hide.

The best and most economical suppliers of high quality leather in small quantities are the jobbers of garment,

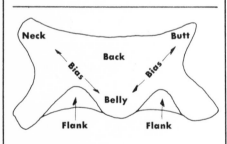

bag, and belt leathers located in the leather districts of large cities. Craftpeople and leather shops usually deal with the leather-district tradesmen. Look in the classified directory of the largest city near you, under the listing "Leather."

Individual leather shops are geared to marketing their own products and are not always willing to sell skins. Most often they sell their scraps already packaged. These packages are something of a gamble, and often the contents are pieces too small to finish a project, or scraps of poor quality are included.

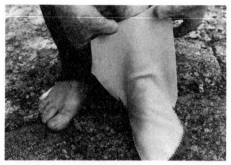

28: The top of the vamp piece should be about three inches wide. It should taper smoothly from points shown as C and D in figure **J**.

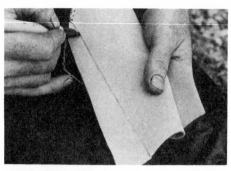

29: Marking side edges of the vamp prior to trimming. Note the awl-pierced front edge of the vamp piece. Line shows vamp tapering to a three-inch-wide top.

30: The back piece is now attached to the sole, slightly overlapping the edge of the vamp. Fold outer back-piece flap over vamp first, then inner flap.

31: If the outside flap of the back piece is too long, cut it down to a reasonable, or comfortable, length. The photograph illustrates this process.

Working the Back Piece

The back piece is simple to make and to attach. With a tape, measure from A to B (figure **J**) around the heel. Using this measurement, make a brown-paper pattern as sketched in figure **J**. Notice that the back piece is slightly curved at the heel. After tracing the pattern on leather for the back piece, cut it out and measure a 4-to-5-foot length of thread.

Center the back piece at the rear of the sole, figure **J**. Begin at center, reserving half the thread for the other side of the seam. Stitch A_1, B_1 to points A and B, and then tie off (figure **I**). Parts of the seam, where the back piece overlaps the vamp, will require a little more force to pull thread through. Use pliers if necessary. When the seam is completed, backstitch the drawstring ends, left over from the puckering process, inside the moccasin, and clip off.

Trimming and Finishing the Back

The back-piece flaps affect the fit of the moccasin, so trim them carefully. Figure K shows where to trim the back piece to join the vamp; trim from points A to E, and the matching points on other side. Put on the moccasin and fold the outside flap of the back piece over the vamp, as in photograph 30. If this flap is too long (it tucks down into the sole), cut off the end, as shown in photograph 31. Now fold the other flap over it.

Stretch a string tightly across the instep from point E, in figure **K** to the matching point on the opposite side of the moccasin, corresponding to point E. Both flaps should be trimmed so that their lower edges fall along the line delineated by the string. Next, from scrap leather cut a lace 1/8 inch wide and about 18 inches long. With your matte knife, make lacing holes an inch above the sole seam. Each pair of lacing holes should be far enough back so the lace will cross the flaps. See photographs 32 and 33. Notch the upper flap as shown in photograph 34.

High-Top Version of the Apache Moccasin

Here is a variation on this basic design actually used by the Apache. The following instructions refer to figure L.

Sole Piece: Identical to that for the low-cut moccasin.

Vamp Piece: Same as short version, but when you have traced the pattern as far as C_1 and D_1 —figure G, page 114 (marked as X and Y on figure L here)— the side edges are parallel.

Back Piece: Rectangular. The width is equal to distance C_1 and D_1, figure L, measured around the heel, with an extra inch or so added for a margin of error, to give leeway when you are attaching back to sole. Unneeded material will be trimmed off.

The following sequence is suggested for making the high-top version:

Make sole, as before.

Attach vamp, as before, to C_1 and D_1, figure L, around toe.

Using the glover's stitch, figure M, attach the vamp at Y, figure L, to the back piece at C_2, and sew up the side to T and U.

Starting at C_2, sew bottom of the back piece to the sole.

When this seam meets the other side of the vamp, at X, trim off the unused portion of the margin-of-error material.

Turn the moccasin inside out, and sew the remaining side seam, from X and D_2 to S and V.

Cut off the top edge so that it is even, and fold down inside to make a hem, if desired.

Traditional Indian ceremonial moccasins were decorated with quillwork or beading. You may wish to imitate these intricate techniques by adapting information and designs in the beadwork section.

Lassie putting the last stitches on a pair of high-top moccasins. Frequent fittings while the moccasins are being made guarantee a comfortable fit.

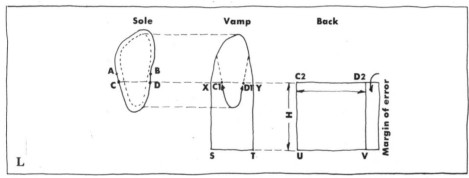

Figure L: Steps in making the high-top moccasin parallel steps for low-top version. Distance between C_1, D_1, measured around the heel, equals distance C_2, D_2.

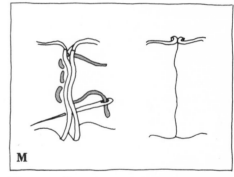

Figure M: Glover's stitch for high-top style.

32: Laces for your moccasins are cut ⅛-inch wide from scrap leather. They should be about 18 inches long. Lacing holes are made in pairs and lie an inch above sole seam.

33: The lace must pass over both back-piece flaps, holding them securely in place. Here, the upper flap is marked for notching, which will keep flaps from shifting.

34: View of the notch being cut to keep moccasin flaps in place. Notch is cut into the upper flap beneath the area where the lace will pass.

Magic with Stitchery

Crewel embroidery is one of the most ancient forms of embroidery, dating back to the fifth-century B.C. in Egypt. A colorful and demanding needlecraft, it derives its name from the use of a special crewel yarn. This is a fine wool yarn with a slight sheen that usually comes in the form of two plies tightly twisted together to form a single strand. A strand can be used singly for delicate effects or many strands can be combined for bolder designs. Traditionally, embroidery is not considered to be crewelwork if worked in a different yarn. There is a durable quality to crewels and they have been widely used for household and personal accessories; coverlets, curtains, clothing, chair seats, cushions, and rugs may be worked in this medium.

None of the stitches used in crewel embroidery are exclusively "crewel" stitches, so the beginning embroiderer will discover it is easy to go on to other techniques, using these stitches as the starting point. In addition, the nature of crewel embroidery allows for individual interpretation, whether the design is completely original or not.

The sampler opposite is my interpretation of a traditional design that provides a good introduction to crewelwork. This sampler includes 36 of the embroidery stitches typically found in contemporary American crewelwork.

*Mildred J. Davis is an internationally known author (*The Art of Crewel Embroidery, Early American Embroidery Designs*), lecturer, teacher, and research authority on textiles. She is Consulting Curator of the Textile Resource and Research Center, Valentine Museum, Richmond, Va., where she organizes and directs its Assemblies for Embroiderers. Most recently she conducted its first International Assembly at Sea. She lives in Chestnut Hill, Mass.*

Crewel embroidery sampler

Materials

Background fabrics: The sampler was worked on linen twill with single 2-ply strands of crewel yarn. Traditionally, crewel is worked on linen, linen twill, cotton and linen woven together, wool, or silk. Today, we also use handwoven linen, silk, denim, and textured fabrics, including synthetics and burlap. The durable, firm weave of linen and silk anchors the stitches while permitting easy passage for the needle and thread.

Yarns: The crewel yarns (sometimes called threads) used in the sampler can be found in beautiful gradations of color. Made by American as well as European firms, they vary in weight, size, twist, and appearance. Synthetic yarns with many of the qualities of crewel wool yarns are available. In general, choose a yarn according to the fabric you are using. Loosely woven, coarse fabrics are usually worked with two or three strands of wool used simultaneously. Tightly woven, fine fabrics usually call for a single strand. Try sample stitches on the fabric for a crewelwork piece to judge the number of strands to use.

Needles: The sampler was worked with a No. 22 chenille needle. Selection of the proper needle is important. Needle sizes must be correlated to fabric weave and yarn. The needle must be slightly larger than the yarn to permit the yarn to go through the fabric without fraying. Crewel and chenille needles, both pointed, are used for crewelwork. Crewel needles, sold in sizes 1 to 10, are about 1¾ inches long, with an easy-to-thread ⅛-inch eye. Popular sizes are 3, 4, and 5 (the smallest of the three sizes). Chenille needles are about 1½ inches long, with a ¼-inch eye. Popular sizes are 20, 22, and 24 (the smallest). When working stitches such as the Whipped or Woven Spider Web (page 123), use a tapestry needle. The blunt end will not pick up the fabric or split your threads.

This enlarged photograph shows a crewelwork sampler designed by Mildred Davis. The traditional motifs are done in muted tones of crewel yarn on linen twill. Instructions for the 36 embroidery stitches used here are given on pages 122–125.

EMBROIDERY CRAFTNOTES: PREPARATION AND TECHNIQUES

Threading the needle and handling yarn lengths

Cut yarn 18 to 24 inches long; a longer strand might fray by the time you reach its end. To thread the yarn: Fold back a few inches of yarn at one end of strand to make a loop.

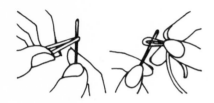

Pull loop taut around the head of the needle (above, left), and pinch this fold with thumb and forefinger. Slip loop off needle and push the pinched fold through the eye of the needle (above, right).

Starting and finishing yarn

When making a hanging, the first length of yarn may be knotted; but most embroiderers anchor the first strand of yarn by making four tiny running stitches (the last of these secured by a back stitch) in a spot that is to be covered with embroidery. To end a length of yarn and to begin subsequent threads, weave them under a few adjacent stitches on the wrong side.

Working with a hoop

Each time the needle is inserted, it goes in vertically with a jabbing motion. Keep one hand above the standing floor hoop and the other below it, as shown in the drawing.

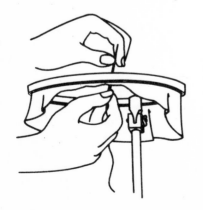

Other accessories: A small, sharp pair of embroidery scissors; a thimble; and an embroidery frame or hoop. Hoops, which are sold in many sizes and styles, such as hand-held or standing floor hoops, stretch the fabric and help you make uniform, unpuckered stitches.

Methods

Transferring the pattern: The first step in making the sampler is to transfer the embroidery pattern to the background material. You will need tracing paper; dressmaker's carbon paper; soft and hard lead pencils; straight pins; and a piece of sturdy, flat-surfaced fabric measuring at least 13-by-11½ inches (to allow a 2-inch margin on all sides for blocking—the shaping process—and framing). I used a linen twill, but a round-thread, Belgian, or Irish linen may be substituted. Place a sheet of tracing paper over the actual size pattern on the opposite page. With a soft pencil, trace the design, omitting numbers and names. Place the linen, right side up, on a table; center the tracing, penciled side up, over it. Pin paper to fabric margins with pins pointing outward; pin around three sides only, leaving one side open. Insert the carbon paper, carbon side down, between tracing paper and fabric. With a dull, hard lead pencil, trace the entire design onto the fabric; lift up the open side occasionally, to see how well the carbon is transferring. Remove pins and papers.

Making the sampler: The sampler pattern opposite has two main elements: a border of blocks of embroidery stitches, and a central motif using most of the stitches employed in the border blocks. It is a good idea to work the border blocks first, to become familiar with the stitches, before you undertake the central motif. The directions for the sampler border are given on pages 126–129, and are divided into two sections. Pages 126 and 127 describe the making of the top portion of the border; pages 128 and 129, the bottom. Each block within the border is shown enlarged for clarity and is described in detail with a key to the names on the pattern on the opposite page. The numbers in the text refer to the corresponding numbers used in the sequential stitch instructions (pages 122 to 125).

The large central motif includes most of the stitches used in the border blocks. The stitches for this section are identified by their sequential numbers on the pattern on the opposite page; use the picture on page 119 as a guide for color. Begin the central motif by working the easiest stitches first, those lowest in the numerical sequence, and then progress to the more difficult stitches.

Colors are indicated in the text, but if you wish to change the color scheme of the sampler, choose yarn in a color suited to your decor, and with four or five color gradations available. Do not hesitate to experiment with color, but do strive for a balance of colors throughout the design; avoid isolated areas worked in a single color, especially one that is very bright.

In the lower right-hand corner of the finished sampler, write your name, and the date with a laundry marking pen and then embroider over the signature and date in Outline Stitch (4, page 122). When the sampler is completed, wash, press, or block, as necessary, and then mount it. (See Craftnotes, pages 126–127 and 128–129).

Practicing the stitches: Before beginning the sampler, you may find it reassuring to practice the stitches (pages 122–125) on a scrap of linen. The stitches are numbered 1 to 36, each successive stitch building on the skills acquired in the preceding stitches. When practicing, start at stitch 1 and advance in sequence through stitch 36. Many of the illustrations for each stitch show the needle going in and out, in one step, for clarity.

Some stitches require a hand motion similar to that used in sewing and are done easily if the fabric is held loosely in the hand. Stitches that are worked best when the fabric is stretched tautly in a hoop are indicated by the symbol ◫ in the text accompanying the illustrations. For the correct way to embroider these stitches, see the Craftnotes at left, applicable to all forms of embroidery. These also show the proper way to thread the needle, and how to begin and end a yarn length.

Figure A: This is a full-size pattern for the crewelwork sampler pictured on page 119. ▶
Numbers key the 36 stitches; border blocks are keyed with names.

Simple Trellis

Pointed Leaf

Acorn

Tendril

Flower

Cross Stitched Trellis

Heart

Flowers

Two Leaves

Bell

Shells

Ovals

Waves

Cherries

Apple

Leaf

Diagonal Trellis

Trees

Rosebuds

Cat

Cactus

Cross Stitched Diagonal Trellis

A

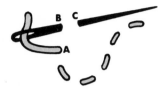

1. Running Stitch: Bring needle up at A, down at B, up at C. Space between stitches should be equal to their length.

2. Straight Stitch 🄷: Worked the same as running stitch, but the stitches are longer. May be worked in rows, at angles, or at random.

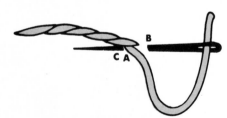

3. Backstitch: Work from right to left. Bring needle up at A; insert at B; bring it up at C, and draw thread through. Go back; insert in front of A, and complete figure. Be sure the stitch lengths are uniform.

4. Outline or Stem Stitch: This is a basic stitch used to embroider lines, outlines and the stems of flowers. Start at top or bottom guide line. Bring needle up at A; insert at B at a slant as shown; bring up at C, and pull yarn through. Always keep the yarn on the same side of the needle.

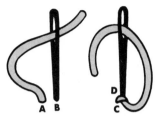

5. Seed Stitch 🄷: Small stitches randomly placed. Come up at A, go down at B, a small distance away. Come up at C and go down at D, crossing the first stitch diagonally.

6. Satin Stitch 🄷: A plump, solidly filled figure is created with this stitch. Outline the area to be worked with small Backstitches (3), to keep the edge even. Come up at A; draw yarn through. Go in at B; pull yarn through. Continue, placing stitches side by side across the design just outside the outline stitches. Keep the stitches close and their direction uniform.

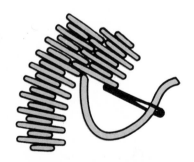

7. Long and Short Stitch 🄷: Resembles Satin Stitch (6) and is used to create a solid filling. Alternate long and short Satin Stitches, as shown, placing them side by side. In the next row, a long stitch goes below a short one.

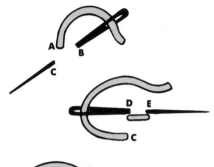

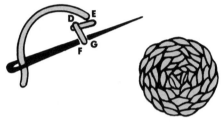

8. Raised Rose 🄷: Bring yarn up at A, and with needle at a slant, go in at B; come up at C; pull yarn through. Go in at D; come up at E; pull yarn through. Go in at F; come up at G; pull yarn through. Work a spiral of Outline Stitches (4) around triangle formed by first three steps.

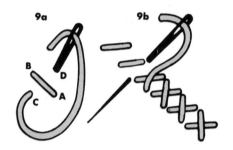

9. Cross Stitch: To make a single Cross Stitch, bring needle up at A; insert at B, up at C, and in at D, as in figure 9a. Be sure B and C, A and D are parallel. To make a row of Cross Stitches, work a row of slanting stitches from right to left, or left to right. Then work back across row, slanting stitches in the opposite direction, as in figure 9b. In a group of Cross Stitches, be sure the top stitches always slant in the same direction.

STITCHES

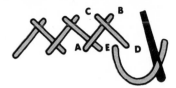

10. Herringbone Stitch: Row of slanted stitches crossed at top and bottom. Following the drawing, bring needle up at A, in at B, up at C, in at D, up at E, and continue.

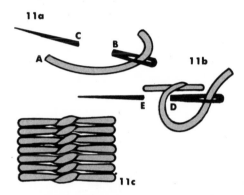

11. Roumanian Stitch: Bring needle up at A; pull yarn through. Go in at B and up at C, with thread below needle as in figure 11a. Pull yarn through. For second part of stitch, insert needle at D; bring out at E (figure 11b). Pull yarn through. Continue as from A. Result is shown in figure 11c.

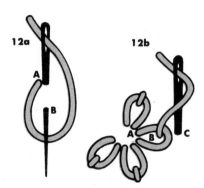

12. Lazy Daisy or Detached Chain: Bring the yarn up at A; make a loop and hold down loop with thumb. Insert the needle back at A and bring it out over the loop at B. Pull yarn through. Next, anchor the loop by inserting the needle at C and pulling the yarn through to the underside. May be worked separately as in figure 12a, but most often worked in a circle to form petals of a flower (figure 12b).

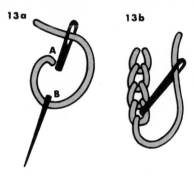

13. Chain Stitch: This stitch is also used for a decorative outline. Bring needle up at A; lay a loop of yarn on the fabric. Hold the loop while you insert the needle back at A and bring point of needle up at B, with loop held under point (figure 13a). Draw yarn through. Form remaining loops in same manner, always inserting needle where it emerged from last stitch (figure 13b). Anchor last stitch of chain by inserting the needle below its loop.

14. Open Chain: Made in the same way as the Chain Stitch (13) except the top of the loop is open. Finish off as for Chain Stitch.

15. Twisted Chain: Same as Open Chain (14), with a twist at the top of the loop.

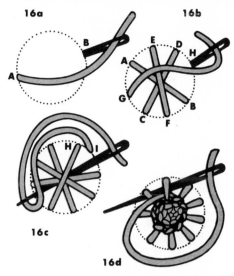

16. Whipped Spider Web ◨: Work spokes with chenille or crewel needle. Bring needle up at A; insert at B, bisecting circle as in figure 16a. Bring needle up at C, pull yarn through and insert at D; up at E, in at F, up at G, and down at H, following figure 16b. Bring needle up at I (figure 16c). Change to tapestry needle. Slide tip of needle under all the threads where they cross at the center and loop the yarn over and under the needle tip as in figure 16c. Tighten yarn, forming a knot at the center, and the ninth spoke. To whip the spider (figure 16d), slide needle counterclockwise under two spokes of yarn (do not catch the fabric); pull yarn through; slide needle back under the second of these spokes and then under the spoke ahead, as shown. Pull yarn through. Continue in a spiral until the circle is filled.

17. Woven Spider Web ◨: This differs from Whipped Spider Web (16) in that the yarn is woven over and under single spokes counterclockwise. Work Whipped Spider to completion of center knot; then weave yarn under first spoke, over second, under third, continuing until circle is filled.

18. Backstitched Chain: Work a row of Chain Stitch; finish off. Using a contrasting color yarn, if desired, Backstitch (3) through it, as shown.

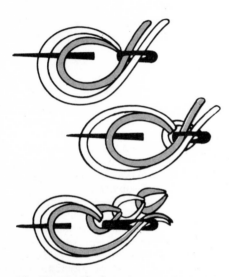

19. Magic Chain: Chain worked with two colors of yarn in the same needle. Thread needle with first and second colors, and proceed as for Chain Stitch (13), but loop only first color under the needle for the first stitch. For the second stitch, loop the second color under the needle. Alternate this pattern in subsequent stitches.

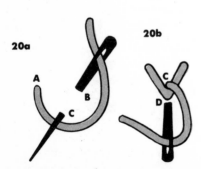

20. Fly Stitch: Like the Lazy Daisy Stitch (12), but open at top. Bring needle up at A; insert at B, and come up at C with the thread looped under the needle, as in figure 20a. Pull yarn through. Insert needle at D (figure 20b) to secure the loop.

21. Open Attached Fly Stitch: Like Fly Stitch (20), but anchored by a long rather than short stitch. Work from top to bottom.

22. Closed Attached Fly Stitch: Worked in the same manner as Open Attached Fly Stitch (21), but with the stitches close together and the connecting loops short.

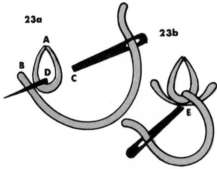

23. Wheat Ear Stitch: Combination of Lazy Daisy Stitch (12) and Fly Stitch (20). Bring needle up at A, form loop of desired size, and reinsert needle at A, as in Lazy Daisy Stitch (12). Bring the needle up at B and draw through. Insert needle at C and come up at D with yarn under needle (figure 23a). Pull through. Anchor at E (figure 23b).

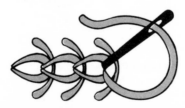

24. Attached Wheat Ear: Complete Wheat Ear (23) through D, but do not anchor at E. Instead, make loop of next Wheat Ear, and then end by anchoring as in Wheat Ear.

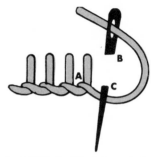

25. Blanket Stitch: Work from left to right. Bring needle up at A. Loop yarn in position shown, insert needle at B with point coming up at C and the yarn looped under needle. Draw yarn through. Repeat B-C across. This stitch can be used as a filling or to form outlines.

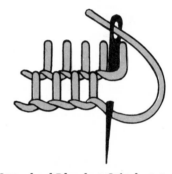

26. Attached Blanket Stitch: Joined rows of Blanket Stitch (25). Work row of Blanket Stitches. Finish off. Starting at the beginning of the row, work second row in bottom loops of first row. Work additional rows the same way.

27. Buttonhole Stitch: A closed Blanket Stitch (25). Proceed as for Blanket Stitch, but space stitches close together, as shown.

STITCHES

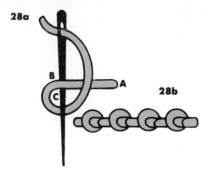

28. Coral Stitch: Series of attached knots. Come up at point A. Hold yarn to the left; go in at point B, and come up at C with yarn under the needle. Draw knot tight. Lay thread to the left for next stitch. Continue as for B and C. Figure 28b shows a row of completed Coral Stitches.

29. French Knot: Come up at the point where the French Knot is to be. Form loop around needle, and insert needle vertically into or just next to same point. Pull loop tight around needle. Hold yarn with left thumb, pull needle through (figure 29a). Figure 29b shows enlarged finished French Knot.

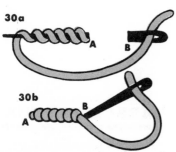

30. Bullion Stitch: Bring needle up at A. Insert needle at B and bring out near A; do not pull needle all the way through. Twist thread 6 times around point of needle as in figure 30a (the coils, when pushed together, should equal the distance between A and B). Holding coils and needle securely with thumb and forefinger, draw needle through fabric and coils. Carefully pull thread to tighten stitch so knot lies flat against the fabric (knot will flip over). Reinsert needle in B (figure 30b).

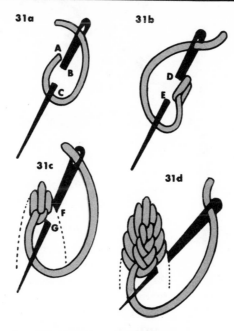

31. Closed Cretan Stitch: Closely spaced, elongated loops that overlap. Work from top to bottom. Bring the needle up at A, in at B, and up at C with the yarn looped under the needle (figure 31a). Pull yarn through. Insert needle at D, and come up at E with yarn under the needle as in figure 31b. Pull yarn through. Next stitch, F to G (figure 31c), will begin just below and to the right of B. Pull yarn through, and continue. Increase the length of the stitches as you work downward (figure 31d).

32. Open Cretan Stitch: Same as Closed Cretan Stitch (31), but with space between them.

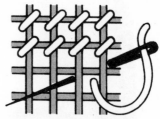

33. Simple Trellis ▣**:** Trellises are squared filling stitches and consist of a combination of couching with preceding stitches. To couch means to tack down long threads with small stitches. Use long Straight Stitches (2) to lay evenly spaced trellises of yarn across area to be worked. Then couch intersections with small diagonal stitches as shown here.

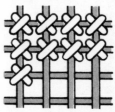

34. Cross Stitched Trellis ▣**:** Worked as Simple Trellis (33), except the yarn is couched at intersections with small Cross Stitches (9).

35. Simple Diagonal Trellis ▣**:** Lay vertical and horizontal yarns as in Simple Trellis (33). Then lay diagonal yarns. Couch intersections with small diagonal stitches.

36. Cross Stitched Diagonal Trellis ▣**:** Lay yarns as in Simple Diagonal Trellis (35). Work diagonal rows of Outline Stitch (4), slanting in opposite direction from the first diagonals. Couch with Cross Stitches (9) where diagonals intersect.

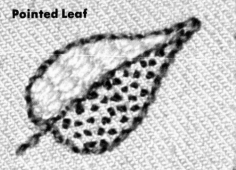

Simple Trellis

Pointed Leaf

Acorn

Heart

Flowers

Two Leaves

Upper left-hand corner of sampler.

The stitches used for the border of the top of the sampler are given on these two pages. To follow the instructions, start in the lower left corner of this page and work your way up and around the border in a clockwise direction. Methods of making the numbered stitches are given on pages 120 through 125.

Two Leaves: Both leaves are done in Cretan Stitch: the light green leaf is Closed Cretan Stitch (31); the dark green one is Open Cretan Stitch (32), and edged in Chain Stitch (13).

Flowers: French Knot (29) flowers are in four gradated shades of blue, light to dark. Stems are Outline Stitch (4) in blue.

Heart: Outer edge of heart is worked in Blanket Stitch (25) in light blue. Center is filled with rows of red Attached Blanket Stitch (26).

Simple Trellis: Each corner of the sampler is worked in a variation of this basic couched trellis, Simple Trellis (33). The trellis yarns are light green; the little couching stitches are light blue. The entire outside border of the sampler is worked in dark green Twisted Chain Stitch (15). The blocks are separated by Outline Stitch (4) in medium light blue. The inner border is worked in Chain Stitch (13) in medium blue.

Pointed Leaf: The shape of the leaf is delineated in medium blue Backstitch (3) as is the leaf's vein. Solid rows of light blue Backstitch fill the leaf's upper area. Lower half of the leaf is filled with dark green Seed Stitches (5).

EMBROIDERY CRAFTNOTE

Washing and Pressing: If finished embroidery is soiled, wash with mild soap flakes in lukewarm water. Roll in a towel and let dry. Place face down on thick towel, cover with damp pressing cloth, and press with warm iron. If fabric still appears puckered, block as directed at right.

To Block Embroidery: Use a soft wood board larger than the piece to be blocked. Place a piece of aluminum foil the size of the background fabric on the board. This prevents the wood from staining the fabric, prevents water absorption, and serves as a pinning guide. Stretch the fabric taut over the foil and tack it to the board with rustproof thumbtacks or pushpins, placed at 1-inch intervals around the four sides.

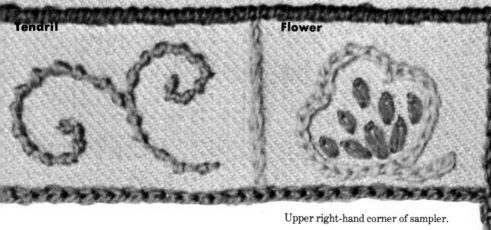

Tendril **Flower**

Upper right-hand corner of sampler.

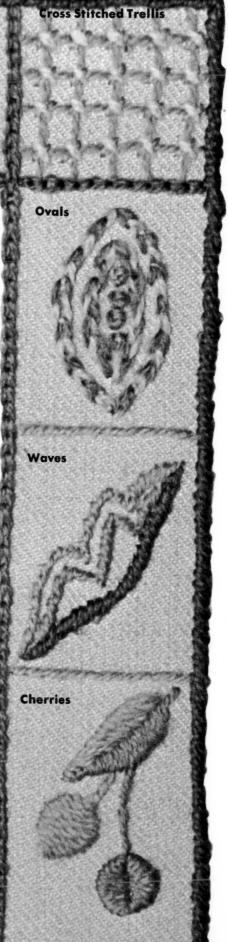

Ovals

Waves

Cherries

Acorn: Left side of acorn is worked in Running Stitch (1); right side and stem are in Straight Stitch (2). Yarn colors are two shades of gold.

Tendril: Curling tendril is worked entirely in Coral Stitch (28) in medium green yarn.

Flower: A delicate flower, outlined in Chain Stitch (13) worked in pink yarn, encircles a group of Lazy Daisy Stitches (14) worked in medium rose yarn.

Cross Stitched Trellis: This block is worked in Cross Stitched Trellis (34). The couched horizontal yarns are light green; the intersections are couched by Cross Stitches (9) with medium blue lower stitches and light blue upper stitches.

Ovals: Lines of inner and outer oval are embroidered in Magic Chain (19) with dark green and yellow yarns. Four dark green French Knots (29) fill the center.

Waves: The figure is worked in Twisted Chain (15) in light and dark greens.

Cherries: Leaf halves are worked in Satin Stitch (6) in two shades of gold. Cherry at right, also in Satin Stitch, is dark gold, one at left in Long and Short Stitch (7). The stems are Outline Stitch (4).

FINISHING

Work across the top, pulling fabric taut and true as you tack, then tack the left side from top to bottom; across lower edge and then up the right side. With cold water and a clean sponge, saturate the embroidery and background. Press paper toweling on it to remove excess water. Allow to dry, away from heat and sunlight, for 24 hours. Unpin.

First Method

This is probably the simplest way to hang a piece of embroidery. For this method you will need a needle and thread or sewing machine, wooden doweling, and a length of yarn (optional). First, trim the background fabric if the edges are uneven. Make narrow hems at the sides by turning the edges under ¼ inch twice. Stitch a hem about 1 inch wide (the size depends upon the thickness of the dowel) at the top, leaving ends open (figure A). Cut a length of dowel about 2 inches longer than the width of the hanging, and insert in hem. Attach a length of yarn to the dowel at the top (figure B) or simply suspend embroidery from the dowel itself. If it is hanging smoothly, make a narrow hem at bottom. If you find that the hanging is curling or buckling, add weight to it by sewing another wide hem at the bottom and inserting another dowel.

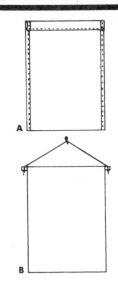

The stitches used for the border of the bottom of the sampler are given on these two pages. To follow the instructions, start at left and work your way down and around in a counter clockwise direction. Methods of making the numbered stitches are given on pages 120 through 125.

Bell: The bell is embroidered in Open Chain (14) in three shades of gold. The hanger is dark gold Chain Stitch (13); the clapper is Satin Stitch (6).

Shells: All four shell-like forms are worked in Buttonhole Stitch (27) in three shades of blue.

Diagonal Trellis: Another variation of a couched trellis, Diagonal Trellis (35). The horizontal and vertical yarns are dark green, the diagonals are dark rose. The couching stitches are gold.

Trees: Both figures are worked in Attached Fly Stitch; the light green tree is Closed Attached Fly Stitch (22); the dark green tree is worked in Open Attached Fly Stitch (21), with the stitches becoming progressively larger.

Rosebuds: Five rosebuds in shades of pink and rose. Clockwise starting from top left: pink, worked in Buttonhole Stitch (27); medium rose in Whipped Spider Web (16); medium rose in Woven Spider Web

Lower left-hand corner of sampler.

MOUNTING

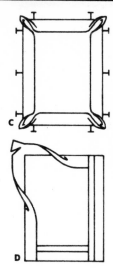

Second Method

To frame an embroidery you need: a frame; a piece of heavy cardboard or composition board (⅛ to ¼ inch thick) cut ⅛ to ⅜ inch smaller than the opening at the back of the frame (to allow room for embroidery fabric); heavy straight pins; and a good, cloth-backed adhesive tape (1½ inches wide). Place embroidery face down on a flat surface, and center the board on top. Fold fabric margins to the back, and insert straight pins into each side to secure fabric temporarily (figure C). Check to make sure that the threads of the fabric are even with the edges of the board. Tape top and bottom edges of the fabric to the board; trim fabric at corners if it seems too bulky; then tape down the sides (figure D). For more permanent mounts, sew rather than tape the margins. Use heavy, rug sewing thread to lace the top and bottom margins together, and the two side margins together. Draw thread taut to lace evenly from one side to the other.

(17); dark rose in Woven Spider Web (17); medium rose in Raised Rose (8). Dark gold stem is Coral Stitch (28). Dark green snippet is Twisted Chain Stitch (15).

Cat: Three dark blue Wheat Ear Stitches (23) and a row of medium blue Attached Wheat Ears (24) flank a light blue cat in Coral Stitch (28) with Fly Stitch (20) ears and paws.

Cactus: Each spiky tip is a Bullion Stitch (30) in two shades of gold. The stems are Coral Stitch (28).

Cross Stitched Diagonal Trellis: The most complex of the corner trellises is Cross Stitched Diagonal Trellis (36). The horizontal and vertical yarns are dark green; the diagonals are light green with dark rose Cross Stitches (9) at the intersections.

Leaf: Each half of the leaf is worked in Herringbone Stitch (10); the left side is medium blue and the right side is dark green. The center line is a row of Backstitched Chain (18) in medium blue and gold. Embroider the outline of the leaf in Chain Stitch (13) with dark green on the right side; in Outline Stitch (4) with medium blue on the left.

Apple: Roumanian Stitch (11), in three shades of rose, is worked in three rows to fill the apple. Stem, in aqua, is done in Chain Stitch (13).

Lower right-hand corner of sampler.

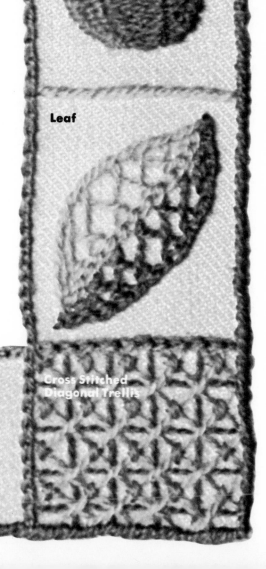

Apple

Leaf

Cross Stitched Diagonal Trellis

Cat

Cactus

PERIOD COSTUMES
From Rags To Riches

Jan Fairservis is a theater costume designer and an illustrator of books on anthropology and physiology. She illustrated Margaret Mead's People and Places *and* Costumes of the East, *written by her husband, Walter A. Fairservis. She has designed numerous costumes for theater and now designs for The Sharon Playhouse in Sharon, Conn.*

Costumes have been with mankind all through recorded history. A cave painting discovered in France shows a sorcerer in a costume of deerskin and horns; neolithic frozen graves in Siberia preserved ceremonial costumes decorated with felt and fur. Archaeologists believe religious ceremonies, tribal rituals, pageants and festivals were always conducted in appropriate costumes. Theater, which developed from ancient religious rites, has preserved the use of costumes, setting them apart from everyday clothes by exaggerations or distortions of what is familiar, by historical holdovers from former times and by exotic representations from distant lands or magical epochs.

The Magic of Costume
More popularly, costumes are associated with a foreign land or with the past, even one's own family past. Grandmother's gown can become the costume for a birthday ball or a school drama presentation. Everyday clothes are manifestations of the wearer, but when you don a costume you relinquish your own personality for the moment and accept garments appropriate to a new role. Perhaps this is why costumes have always been so compelling. They do seem to have a magical effect on the wearer as well as the observer. In a costume, you may find a new freedom.

My family loves to take part in plays, pageants, and festivals. Frequently we do not want to invest in the rental of theatrical costumes or to buy the many yards of fabric needed to make them. There is a way out of this dilemma. On the next pages are ways of making costumes of all kinds from materials that are easy to come by, and from each of the three examples, dozens of variations are possible.

Finding Raw Materials
Start by looking through thrift shops and Salvation Army stores for old evening gowns, bedspreads, curtains, draperies, and fabric remnants. Upholstery and fashion-fabric stores occasionally have sales where interesting yardage is sold at reduced prices. Attics often harbor old dresses, men's outdated formal clothes, old ballet tights, hats and gloves.

Actually, almost anything can become a costume or an accessory to a costume. Brown paper bags can be recycled into Halloween goblin costumes or cowboy-and-Indian outfits as shown on pages 132 and 133. Old clothing from the past (page 134) is easy to recycle into great costumes for a play, a party or some other special event. From the principle of the one-dress pattern (page 135) you can make all kinds of costumes. The caftan, page 136, can be a starting point for many variations, as can any of the period costumes on page 137.

Make-Up and Make Believe
But your "costume" does not end with the clothing. Hair style, hair cut, wigs, beards, and mustaches are essential parts of the total effect you are considering. And so, of course, is make-up. Materials that were once available only to professional make-up artists can now be found at many cosmetic counters.

Use your imagination and experiment to achieve a number of different effects—character faces, masks, youth or old age.

Starting with the examples of costume shown here, you can develop all kinds of marvelous creations.

Teviot Fairservis, Jan's 19-year-old daughter, wears a Restoration costume made from two thrift shop evening dresses. Panniers that spread the skirt are described on page 134.

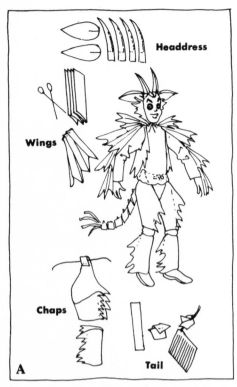

Figure A: This goblin costume is made of paper bags. The jagged cutting on the edges of each part and the pleated wings give it a weird, devilish look.

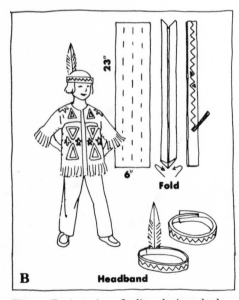

Figure B: American Indian designs look good on buckskin-colored (grocery bag) paper. Headband is folded into strips as shown, decorated, then stapled or glued.

Beth's goblin costume was not cut to a precise pattern. The pieces were cut and stapled together to fit her. Strings secure horns, sleeves, chaps, and tail.

Paper costumes

With paper, scissors, a stapler, masking tape, string, and cardboard, wild headdresses and costumes can be made. My daughter, Beth, was a goblin in a costume made from eight paper bags. Headdress with cardboard horns and ears taped together, has paper sideburns. Wings were pleated, cut, spread, and stapled to the paper sleeves. Chaps, attached to a string belt, were in two pieces so Beth could run. Tail started with a paper tassel; then links of cut paper were twisted and stapled up the string. Wings were tied on with string across the shoulders, and a matching sweater hid most of the strings. Making the jacket on the opposite page is a simple project a child can share.

Children have fun making and decorating a paper-bag jacket like the one at right.

1: Cut bottoms off two paper bags. Cut bags open at the seam. Fold one bag in half lengthwise for yoke and sleeve piece. Cut other bag in half vertically to form back. Cut other half in half again vertically to form the two front pieces.

2: Cut semicircle to fit neck at center of yoke fold. Cut V-shaped front opening.

There is enough paper in only two large grocery bags to make a jacket of Indian (or other) design for a seven-year-old. Use big scissors to cut the bags, following the photographs on this page. It's easier if you work on a large area, like the floor. After you have cut the bags you can staple them together in a matter of minutes. I like a hand-held stapler, but a table type can be used. For decorating, the colors of crayons, felt-tip pens or poster paints show up well on this paper. Indian or peasant motifs or abstract designs created by the child hold special appeal.

3: After placing a front piece on yoke front at opening, attach top of front to bottom of yoke with staples, 3 inches apart, forming ½-inch seam. Repeat.

4: Staple bottom of sleeves after fronts are folded down and seams flattened. Omit underarm staples. Attach back in same manner. Staple front pieces to the back.

You may want to outline coloring areas on the first jacket you and your child make, to teach a traditional design. The author did these scallops and flowers.

1840

conservative
1840–1900

1890's
dandy

Puritan

C

Thrift-shop finds

The basic shape of men's clothes has not changed so very much in the past century. Most of the changes have been in details—buttons, cuffs, lapels, jacket lengths, pocket flaps, and shoulder lines. Women's clothes have varied more radically, but the Restoration costume on page 131 is an illustration of what can be done with an old evening dress. Such historic costumes depend on underskirt supports.

Dressing Up for 1840

In the early 1800s a man was expected to wear a wide, colorful scarf, or a stock, and a very high collar. This romantic style of dress was adopted by English gentlemen as well as dandies, and was eventually accepted everywhere in Europe and America. Later on, during the Victorian age, men began to wear collars and ties similar to those used today.

The costume (figure C) of a young man of the 1840s consists of a jacket from a 1950s natural-shoulder suit of beige gabardine. Darts added front and back shaped a low, tight waistline. The pants were decuffed and narrowed, then steam ironed without a crease. Straps that go under the shoes hold the trouser legs at the instep. The collar was covered with velveteen. The waistcoat is plaid taffeta salvaged from an old evening dress. The tie is black silk. A girl's broad-brimmed, natural-straw hat with a black ribbon makes an acceptable hat.

◄Figure C: Thrift-shop men's suits are the basis for these period costumes. Pants may be narrowed or cut off, lapels reset, buttons changed to alter the style. The text describes how some of these costumes were made.

▶ Figure D: Panniers for the Restoration costume pictured on page 131 are made of paper bags stuffed with newspaper and stapled to a tape around the waist. A bustle at the back or a farthingale that encircles the hips under the skirt can be made this way instead of using devices of wire and tape.

D

A Somber Suit for 1620

The Puritans, 1620 to 1700, were poorly dressed compared with the Colonists in southern towns and New York. Because of their religious beliefs, the Puritans avoided gaudy elaborate dress, wearing costumes that had somber colors and simple lines. The Puritan costume can be copied by using a 1940s suit with wide leg pants and a long jacket, still available secondhand. This suit was a gray wool sharkskin with some of the effect of hand-woven fabric. New darts front and back made the jacket fit close to the chest and appear high-waisted. Shoulder seams were slit, and a fold of fabric replaced the pads and stood out, as in the Colonial period. Large snaps and eight to ten buttons up the front, wide white collar and deep cuffs gave the jacket an authentic look. The pants were cut off two inches below the knee. Heavy matching ribbon, long enough to be tied at the side, was sewed to each pant leg. Lines of buttons up the sides added another authentic touch. Gray knee socks, black shoes, and a Boy Scout ranger style hat, sprayed black, finished this costume.

Basic one-dress pattern

Making costumes for children or adults to wear in a play or a pageant, or to a fancy-dress party, is a pleasant kind of sewing because the garments do not need finely finished details—the costume's line is the most important thing to achieve. It takes much less time if you work with a basic dress or dress pattern that fits the person. Besides, an impatient subject usually will not stand still long enough for you to cut and fit a muslin pattern. Start with a simple classic dress, robe, or suit, and modify it to look like a picture of the costumed character. Figure E shows how a basic dress for a little girl can be varied.

The basic-dress pattern (figure E) had puff sleeves and a long skirt cut in four pieces. This was particularly adaptable because it didn't have a seam up the front. The dress could be belted very high with a ribbon to make a Kate Greenaway or an Empire costume.

Dressing a Princess, Peasant and Queen

To make a Renaissance costume for a little princess—the Snow White dress—the bodice fullness was stitched to a stiffened underbodice. A curved belt gave the deep, pointed bodice line needed; the belt was cut from cardboard and covered with fabric. The ruff was made of three circles of organdy (center circle 1-inch radius, large circle 8-inch radius) slit on the straight of the material, and the three were sewed together. Then they were pleated like a fan and sewed to a ribbon, which anchored the ruff to the dress and protected the back of the neck. The skirt was lifted away from the hips by a farthingale, made of small paper bags as seen in figure D. Long, narrow sleeves were added.

The basic dress became a peasant costume for an operetta with the addition of embroidered tape. A great variety of embroidered ribbons and tapes is available in fabric stores because these decorations have become so fashionable. The tape was sewed around the neckline and as cuffs on the puff sleeves. You can trim the apron with it, or perhaps sew several narrow bands on a shorter skirt to go over the basic dress. This overskirt should be a bright, plain color. If you are making many peasant outfits, fancy tapes might be too expensive; bias strips of patterned cloth could be used instead. The once-popular lace-trimmed crinolines have been preserved in many attics; one of these can add fullness and bounce to the skirt. Fitted boots are handsome with a peasant costume; but tights and ballet shoes are good, too.

The medieval costume for a girl playing a queen in a fairy tale is worn over a contrasting-color turtleneck knit shirt. The sash, almost three yards long, was made of silky brocade. The headdress was made in three layers. First, a bright silk kerchief, covering part of the forehead, was tied around the head. Then a white wimple was wound under the chin and secured on top of the head. Finally, a light silk veil, long enough to hang to the hips, was pinned on top, to float behind the wearer. A small crown was cut from cardboard and stapled together. Then it was shellacked, and painted gold.

Boned undergarments, hoops or wire frameworks, and many petticoats added to the weight and grandeur of women's clothing until the age of central heating and liberation began in this century. Even children in advanced European countries were confined in tight-fitting bodices and ornate clothing. Today, our children enjoy dressing up in long skirts and big hats, and little girls imitate tight bodices by cinching belts around their waists. Adults have exclaimed over the feeling of elegance given them by the costumes they have worn—high, stiff collars, ruffles and lace, great capes, heavy clothing made of rich fabrics. With a basic knowledge of machine sewing and a pattern as a starting point, you can produce costumes for all occasions that will be worn with great delight.

Basic dress pattern

Renaissance princess

Peasant girl

Medieval queen

E

Figure E: The basic dress was found in an easy-to-sew section of a pattern book. Detail sketches show how belt and ruff were cut for dress adapted for a Renaissance princess; the peasant and the fairy tale queen costumes are also from the same dress.

Caftans

All sorts of costumes, ranging from that of an Asian horseman to that of a Medieval princess, can be made from a caftan pattern. You can buy such a pattern or draw one on newspapers (figure F). Fabric from old bedspreads, blankets, or draperies can be used. The short robe Asian horseman was cut knee length; the arms are raised high when it is belted, so that a deep fold covers the belt. The Asian trousers shown in figure F may be worn under the first four robes. They can be made of sheets. They are very full and are gathered at the waist. A diamond of fabric at the crotch makes them fit better. Shirts can be old ones with the collar removed, worn backward. Hats for the horseman and Cossack may be made of fur cloth; the wise man wears a square of soft cloth held by a wide band; and the magician wears a turban, a long strip of cloth wound about the head. The Renaissance prince wears tights, a short robe with pleated sleeves and pleated short trousers. His velvet hat is cut as a circle and gathered to a headband.

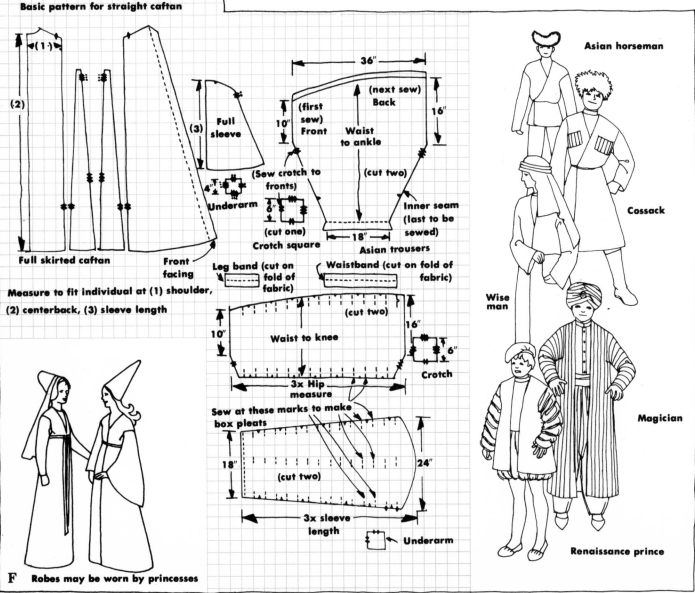

Basic pattern for straight caftan

Fold of fabric — Fold of fabric
Side back — Side front
Sleeve
Underarm square
Turn back front facing
Back — Front

Full skirted caftan

Full sleeve
Underarm
(1) (2) (3)

Measure to fit individual at (1) shoulder, (2) centerback, (3) sleeve length

Asian trousers

36"
10" (first sew) Front — (next sew) Back
Waist to ankle
16"
(cut two)
(Sew crotch to fronts)
4" Underarm
6" Crotch square (cut one)
18"
Inner seam (last to be sewed)

Leg band (cut on fold of fabric)
Waistband (cut on fold of fabric)

(cut two)
10" Waist to knee
16" Crotch 6"
3x Hip measure

Sew at these marks to make box pleats
18" (cut two) 24"
Front facing
3x sleeve length
Underarm

Front facing

F **Robes may be worn by princesses**

Asian horseman
Cossack
Wise man
Magician
Renaissance prince

Figure F: From these basic patterns many costume variations can be devised. See page 158 for instructions on how to enlarge patterns.

Making a period dress

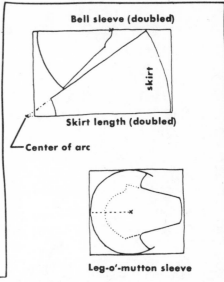

Bell sleeve (doubled)

skirt

Skirt length (doubled)

Center of arc

Leg-o'-mutton sleeve

From any period dress pattern of the type found in most pattern books you can make costumes ranging from the seventeenth to the twentieth century. Adjustments are made in the fit of the bodice, the slope of the shoulder seam, and the way sleeves fit into the armholes. The costumes shown in figure G are simplified, and bodice and skirt are sewed together. The bodice must be lined with strong fabric; boning, often used in evening dresses, is sewed on at the darts front and back. A long zipper up the back makes putting on the bodice quick and easy. Heavy-duty snaps keep strain off the zipper, hold the fold of cloth that hides it and fasten up the back of the skirt.

Figure G shows the decorations characteristic of dresses worn at the dates noted. The 1640 dress has a fan collar (see figure E, page 135), a fabric-covered cardboard triangle in front and added puff sleeves. The 1680 dress needs the collar in the drawing. The 1780 dress is trimmed with box-pleated, 4-inch-wide strips. The high 1830 waistline makes boning unnecessary, but

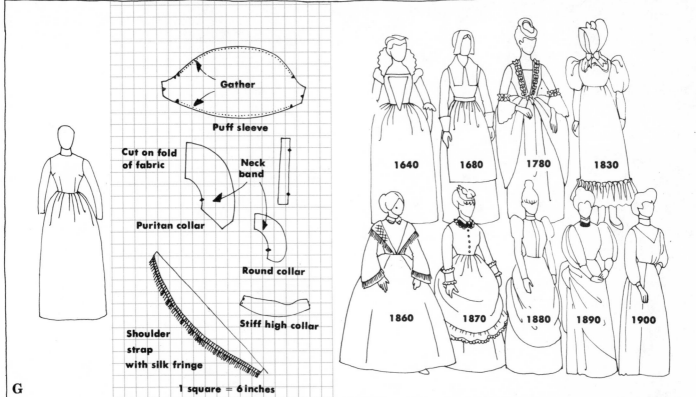

Gather

Puff sleeve

Cut on fold of fabric

Neck band

Puritan collar

Round collar

Stiff high collar

Shoulder strap with silk fringe

1 square = 6 inches

1640   1680   1780   1830

1860   1870   1880   1890   1900

G

large puff sleeves and collar require more fabric. The 1860 bodice has shoulder straps and bell sleeves. The 1880 dress has leg-o'-mutton sleeves. The puff sleeves of 1890 are huge and come below the elbow.

Skirts change the line of a costume radically, but are not as hard to make as bodices. They should be at least 5 yards around the hem, except for the 1830 dress, for which 3 yards will do. The pleated ruffle, however, requires quite a bit of fabric. Although all the skirts are cut in four gores, the angle of the gores varies, because some skirts are gathered at the waist. Dresses of 1780, 1870, 1880, and 1890 have two skirts, draped over a farthingale or bustle, and extra length must be allowed for that.

A skirt is draped by pinning it to a tape around the waist of a model wearing a bustle and petticoat. It is then sewed and attached to the bodice.

Figure G: Bodice and skirt proportions and decorative details differ, but simplified costumes of all these styles from 1640 to 1900 may be built on a basic-dress pattern.

RECANING CHAIRS
New Seats for Chairs

Replacing the woven seat of an elegant old chair seems an impossible home project to many people, I guess. But it isn't. In fact, it really isn't difficult at all. I've taught dozens of people, maybe hundreds, to "bottom" their own chairs. The three projects on the next eight pages will show you, step-by-step, how to weave chair seats of cane, splints, or rush.

The history of chair-seat weaving is obscured in the mists of antiquity. Strips of natural materials like rush, cane, and wooden splints were woven into ground mats many thousands of years ago, archaeologists say. Then came baskets, and I'm sure some prehistoric citizen turned one of them over and sat on it—a kind of woven seat, right? Perhaps someone made a frame of sticks and wove a seat across them. No one knows for sure.

In recent history, woven seats have enjoyed continuous popularity for several hundred years. Sheraton and Chippendale and their many imitators often used rush for seats in their beautiful chairs. In the Victorian Era, people loved the light, crisp look of woven cane. And, of course, country folks have always been partial to hickory and ash splints for the seats of their handmade chairs.

The result is that there are a lot of old chairs around with woven seats that have been broken out or caved in, so you have a great opportunity if you learn how to reweave them.

Warren Bausert is an expert craftsman who has had 20 years of professional experience in caning and reweaving seats for chairs. He is the owner of the Eli Caning Shop in Centereach, N.Y.

Defining Cane, Splints, and Rush

Many people are not clear as to just what cane, splints, and rush are. Cane comes from the outer bark of a certain type of palm tree. It is cut into strips, 1/16- to 3/16-inch wide, and sold in hanks of 1,000 feet—enough to do four chairs. Cost of a hank ranges from $4 to $6 depending on the width and where you buy it.

Splints are simply long, extremely thin strips of wood—traditionally ash or hickory, but now including wood from the same palm that produces cane. Splints are sold by the one-chair bundle.

Rush is made from the common cattail plant, which has leaves up to 7 feet long. The cattail leaves are gathered in August after the plants are full-grown but before the seed heads start to turn brown. The leaves are seasoned under carefully controlled light, temperature, and humidity conditions so that, as they dry, they do not become too brittle. Then they are twisted into strands. In addition to natural rush, there is a type made of kraft paper which looks very much like the real thing. Rush is sold by the pound; it takes 2 to 3 pounds to do one chair.

Tools and Materials

Cane, splints, and rush are available from the same sources, although natural rush and splints are often hard to find. Try local craft supply houses first. Some department stores carry seat-weaving materials. And there are mail order supply houses which often advertise in craft magazines.

Tools you'll need are not unusual: scissors (or shears), tack hammer, tack puller, razor blade, knife, a fine wood rasp, a pan for soaking material, a few spring-type clothespins to clamp loose strands, some old cloth for dampening material, and a narrow, blunt piece of metal for poking and weaving strands. You will also find some special tools that you will need for specific projects mentioned in the project discussion.

The author wove the new cane seat on this attractive maple-and-mahogany chair in a couple of hours. The materials for the job cost about one dollar.

Weaving a splint seat for a chair $\$$ ⬛ 👥 🪣

A splint seat is generally considered appropriate for a chair of simple folk design like the traditional mule-ear chair. Any chair with round rails and stretchers, however, is a candidate for a splint seat.

The splints used for chair seats are usually made from very thin strips of ash or hickory wood, split into strands that are ½-inch, ⅝-inch, or ¾-inch wide. Since lengths vary, splints are sold by the pound or by the bundle. One bundle or 1 pound is enough to bottom an average chair with a seat 16 inches wide. There are other types of splint besides ash and hickory. Flat reed splints are often used instead. Two wider forms of splints, known as flat fiber reed and wide binding cane, can be used for outdoor furniture and certain more sophisticated styles. Whatever the type of splints used, they are all woven in the same way.

Basically, weaving a chair seat is like weaving anything else. You lay down parallel strands, called the warp, in one direction, and insert other strands, called the weft, over and under the warp strands at right angles. Although warp strands may be laid from the front of the chair to the back, in my experience it is easier to lay the warp from side to side. The result should be the same in either case.

Before starting this project, make sure the frame of the chair is in good shape. Remove all old tacks and nails, sand out the scratches, repair any breaks, and apply a new finish, if necessary.

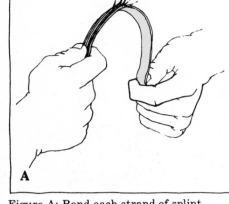

Figure A: Bend each strand of splint, to determine which side should face out. Splinters indicate the wrong side.

1: Tack first soaked strand of the warp to underside of seat rail. Pull the warper, as these strands are called, over rail and across to opposite rail.

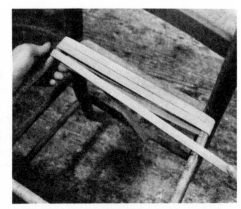

2: Push each strand snugly against the previous strand as you wrap the side rails. Each strand of splint should be soaked 30 minutes or so before using.

3: Use a spring clamp to hold the warper in place while you splice a new strand to it (see figure B). Never splice splints on the top layer or where they turn over the seat rails.

4: When the warp strands are completely laid, clamp the end to a seat rail, but do not cut off the end. Simply tack it, and weave the tail into the seat. Next step is to weave in weft splints.

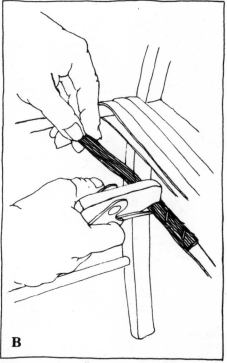

Figure B: Splice the short strands of splint together by overlapping and stapling them as you weave. Splices must fall under seat, where they won't show.

Strands of splint, woven together, make an attractive and sturdy chair seat. Use this photograph as a weaving pattern as you work on the project.

Soak a few splints in water for about 30 minutes, to make them soft and pliable. Coil them for soaking with the nonsplintering side (figure A) facing out. As you remove one splint, put another in to soak, so you will always have a workable supply on hand. Since the strands are comparatively short, you will have to splice each new one to the last strand. A stapler splices well (see figure B), but you can also join splints by notching the edges of both strands and then wrapping them with stout string while they are overlapped. Hide the splices by making them on the bottom layer of splints.

To lay the warp, wrap the strands from side rail to side rail. Start by tacking the first strand (called a warper) to the underside of a rail, leaving four inches or more behind. Bring the warper over the rail, across, and down around the opposite rail. Continue wrapping until the entire seat area is filled. Photographs 1 through 4 show the process of laying the warp. At the finish, clamp the final strand until you have tacked it under the seat rail. Leave about four inches of splint beyond the tack, to be woven into the seat. The seat shown in the photographs took six warpers, spliced together; but seats and splints vary.

Herringbone: 1st row is under 1, over 3, under 3, etc.; 2nd row, under 2, over 3, under 3, etc.; 3rd row, under 3, over 3, under 3, etc.; 4th row, over 1, under 3, over 3, etc.; 5th row, over 2, under 3, over 3, etc.

At age 14, the author learned to weave cane, splints, and rush from his father. Now he is teaching a fourth generation of Bauserts this family enterprise.

The next step is to weave splints across the warpers at right angles. If the seat were a square or a rectangle, this would be a simple matter, but few seats are. Most are wider in front than in back, so it takes more splints to cover the front rail than the back one. For example, the chair in these photographs required 20 splints across the back rail and 24 across the front. So before you start weaving, do a little measuring.

Subtract the length of the back rail from the length of the front rail, and divide the difference in half. Measure in from each end of the front rail by that amount, and make a pencil mark. The area between the pencil marks and the ends of the back rail is a rectangle, and you can weave normally in that area. But outside the pencil marks, there are two triangles, which also must be woven. Start with the right side first.

Take a short strand of splint, round off one end, and weave it through the warpers at the right end of the front rail. Go under one warper, over three, under three, over three, and so on until you reach the side rail (not the back). Keep it parallel to the line between back corner and pencil mark. Start a second strand next to it, but go under two warpers first and then over three, under three, across the seat. Keep adding short splints until you have filled in up to the pencil mark. It usually requires two or three short splints to fill a corner (see photograph 5). Now turn the chair over, and weave the ends of the filler splints into the bottom warp, continuing with the same pattern you used for the filler strands in the top warp. When this is complete, tuck the loose ends, top and bottom, into the center of the seat and tack each strand to the underside of the chair rail (see photograph 7).

Take a full length of splint, and weave it from the pencil mark to the end

5: Weave short splints into front corner first, to square up the rest of the cross-woven strands. This is done because seat is wider at the front than at the back.

6: Underside of chair seat shows how the short corner splints are woven across the bottom and then their ends are buried between the top and the bottom strands.

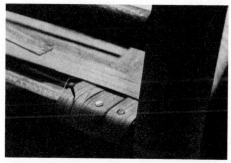

7: Tack all short filler strands to the underside of front rail, to hold them in place. Only the first and the last full-length strands need to be tacked.

8: Weave full-length strands of splint across seat and around back rail. Weave bottom as you did the top. Keep each strand tight against preceding strand.

9: Use a small knife or similar tool to help slip weaving strand between warpers as the seat becomes tight near the finish. End of last strand tucks inside.

of the back rail, keeping it tight against the filler strand. Carefully study the weaving pattern (see color photograph on page 141) before starting to weave. It is three under, three over, continued across, with each new strand starting one warper over. Round off the leading end of each splint to make weaving easier.

After weaving the first strand of splint across to the back rail, tack the other end to the underside of the front rail alongside the filler strands. Bring the first strand around the back rail, and weave it across the bottom in the same pattern. Fill in the entire seat area this way, joining strands on the bottom layer as necessary. When you reach the pencil mark at the other end of the front rail, tuck the end of the strand inside, tack it down, and insert two or three short filler strands, as in the beginning.

The last step is to apply finish to the splint seat. It can be stained like ordinary wood if you want it to match the wood of the chair. Trim off all loose strands first. One popular finish is a mixture of half linseed oil, half turpentine. Let it soak in, then wipe the seat dry. Protect it with shellac or, instead, use any clear, penetrating sealer.

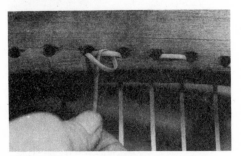

11: In the first step, lay cane from center hole in back rail to center hole in front. Tapered pegs hold cane taut. Reserve back corner hole for diagonals.

12: Tie off cane ends underneath the rails, using this simple knot. After the cane dries, the knot will hold tightly.

13: Complete the vertical cane on the other side of the seat, pegging the ends. The short strands on each side serve to square up pattern in the curved area.

14: Second step starts with horizontal strand laid over vertical strands across back. Don't use corner holes.

Recaning a chair seat

There is never much question as to whether cane is the correct material for repairing the seat of a particular chair. If there is a series of small holes around the seat's perimeter, you can weave a cane seat. If not, you can't. Sometimes broken cane seats are covered by plywood, upholstery, even tin. Turn the chair over, and check the seat rails for cane holes. The fact that a chair once had a cane seat does not necessarily mean the seat can be rewoven. Many chairs have machine-woven cane seats that are glued into grooves. These cannot be rewoven, although the seats can be replaced.

Before you start to recane, get the chair into shape. Remove any seat covering the caning area, repair breaks, cut away any old cane left, clean out the cane holes, and refinish the chair if necessary.

Cane is usually sold in hanks or bunches of about 1,000 feet, which is enough to do four average chair seats. It comes in six sizes, according to strand width. What is called common is the widest cane and is suitable for 5/16-inch cane holes that are about an inch apart. Carriage cane is the thinnest size and is suitable for ⅛-inch holes that are ⅜ inch apart. The four in-between sizes are superfine, fine-fine, fine, and medium. It's a good idea to show the seller a sample of the old cane if you have one. You will also need five or six tapered pegs to hold the cane in place while you work.

To make the cane workable, soak it in lukewarm water for 10 to 20 minutes. Before using a strand, wipe it dry, so the water won't make the wood of the rail swell and decrease the size of the cane holes.

There is a seven-step sequence to weaving a cane seat. You first lace the cane vertically, from rear seat rail to front seat rail. Second, lace the cane horizontally. Third, weave the cane diagonally. Fourth, lay down a second vertical layer. Fifth, weave a second horizontal layer. Sixth, weave a second diagonal layer. Seventh, lace binder cane over the holes. Tie off cane ends beneath the rails as you go (photograph 12).

10: To soften cane, soak it for 10 to 20 minutes in lukewarm water. Do not over-soak; that could discolor the cane and make it more brittle when it dries.

Handwoven cane chair seat has even, octagonal holes when it is done correctly. Use this photograph as a pattern to check your work.

15: Vertical and horizontal canes have been laid and squared up, completing steps one and two. Don't pull too tight.

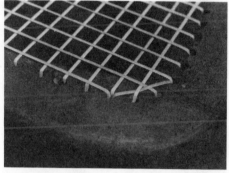

16: In the third step, start the first diagonal at right front corner of the seat. These weavers go under all vertical canes, over horizontal ones.

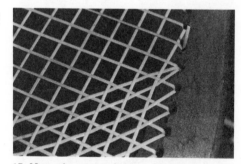

17: Note that two of these diagonal weavers go into the same hole. This is sometimes necessary in curved part of seat rails, to maintain the star pattern.

18: In the fourth step, lay second course of vertical cane over all strands and to right of previous vertical strands.

Step one: Start vertical strands of cane from center hole in back rail to center hole in front rail. Count the holes to be sure. If there is an even number of holes, start with a hole nearest the center. Push about 4 inches of cane through back center hole, and hold it with a wooden peg. Pull cane across and down through the front center hole, making sure the smooth side of the cane faces up. Bring the end of the cane along the underside of the front rail and up through the next hole. Then go across seat to the next hole in the back rail and down through. Then over to the next hole, up through it, across to the front rail, and down through the next hole there. Continue lacing the cane this way until half of the seat is covered (photograph 11). Then cover the other half the same way. Don't pull the cane too tight; it will shrink as it dries. Knot ends as in photograph 12.

Step two: Lace the horizontal strands across from side rail to side rail the same way. These strands lie on top of the vertical ones (photograph 15).

Step three: Weave the first diagonal strands, starting at the right front corner (photograph 16), over horizontal strands and under vertical strands. To maintain six-pointed star pattern, you may need to put two strands through the same hole, because of curvature of side rails (photograph 17).

Step four: Lay a second course of vertical cane over the work thus far, using the same holes as for the first course (photograph 18). This course is not woven in. Lay cane to the right of the original vertical strands.

Step five: Weave in a second course of horizontal strands (photograph 19, page 146), using the same holes as the first course. These strands go under diagonal course and first vertical course, and over second vertical course. Place them to the rear of horizontal strands laid down in step two.

Step six: Weave in a second course of diagonal strands, going in the opposite direction from the first diagonal course (photograph 21, page 146). These weavers always go under all horizontal and over all vertical strands, just the opposite of the way in which diagonal strands were laid down in step three.

Step seven: Fasten the binder cane around the seat's perimeter (photographs 22 through 24 and figure C) to cover the cane holes. Binder cane is usually just cane that is one size wider than the cane you use for weaving. Measure enough to go around.

Good-quality cane is easier to weave because it has no splits or rough eyes.

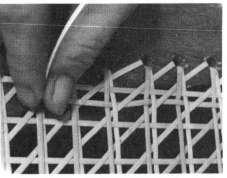

19: In the fifth step, weave second horizontal course across, using the same holes as in step two. Lay these weavers to rear of strands laid in step two.

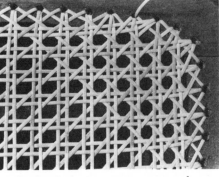

21: In the sixth step, weave a second diagonal strand in the opposite direction from strand in step three. These weavers go under horizontals, over verticals.

20: In tight areas, use an awl or similar tool to lift cane under which a weaver must pass. Do not pull the cane too tight, as it will shrink as it dries.

22: Start binder cane at right rear hole and bring it around perimeter of seat. Loop a strand of weaving cane around it and pull tightly, to hold binder down.

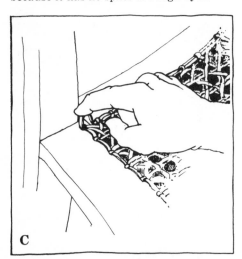

Figure C: Last step in weaving a cane seat is to cover holes and cane ends with binder cane, shiny side up. End of binder is pushed into the starting hole.

Push one end of the binder cane into the corner hole at the right rear corner (photograph 22), and lay out the rest along the back edge of the cane. Select a long strand of weaving cane, and pull all but 4 inches through the hole next to one where binder started. Loop end of weaving cane around binder, and pull it through the same hole, tying the binder down. Then bring the long end of the cane up through the next hole, over the binder, and back down through the same hole. Continue this with each hole until you have tied the binder down all the way around. Tuck the end of the binder into the same hole where you started (figure C).

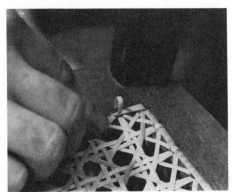

23: To turn a square corner with binder cane, push end of tied strand through corner hole; tie it off; then start new strand of binder, as in the beginning.

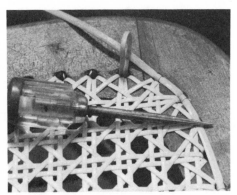

24: Work binder cane around the curved front corner of the chair seat. Keep cane damp and pliable to prevent breaking. An awl helps open up holes.

Making a rush chair seat

A fiber-rush seat is quite easy to make, once you learn to weave your way around. Essentially, it is a matter of taking the rush cord from rail to rail, laying each strand close to the preceding one, until the rails are filled. The rush cord is looped at each corner, under and over one rail and then under and over the rail at right angles to it. Each trip the cord makes around all four corners of the seat is called a bout.

The cord used for this project is fiber rush, which is not the same as real rush. Fiber rush is made of strong kraft paper, twisted into continuous strands. Real rush is made by twisting the leaves of the cattail plant as you weave. I only use real rush when I am restoring a rare antique chair.

This beautifully woven rush seat enhances the style of an antique ladderback chair. The art of rushing is quite easy to learn.

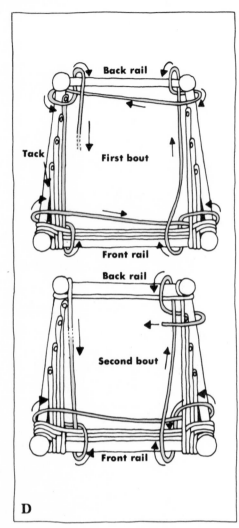

D

Figure D: Looping the corners for a full bout is simple. On the next round (called a bout), you simply repeat the first. Continue weaving this same pattern until the chair seat is filled.

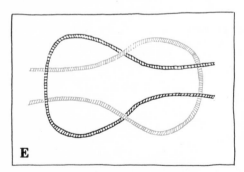

E

Figure E: Square knot for joining strands of fiber rush is done always on underside of seat, where knot won't show. Natural rush is simply twisted together.

Fiber rush is sold by the reel or by the pound. Two pounds will do an average small seat, 3 pounds a large one. Fiber rush comes in different diameters: 3/32, 4/32, 5/32, and 6/32 inch. The two largest sizes are most commonly used, because they fill in more seat area with less work. Some people think the 6/32-inch size looks more like real rush. Fiber rush does not have to be soaked before it is woven.

The first step is to prepare the chair for its new seat. Cut away the old seat and remove any tacks or nails you find. Fill any dents and cracks, repair anything broken, and refinish as needed.

Squaring up the seat

Now you are ready to start weaving the rush cord. If the seat is rectangular or square, you can start right in weaving full bouts. But if the seat is wider at the front than at the back, as most seats are, you have to fill in the front corners to square up the seat. It is very important that all cords cross the rails at right angles; otherwise, there will be a large gap in the center. This means that if it takes 60 cords to fill the back rail, it will take more than 60 to fill the front rail. So you have to add extra filler cords up front. To determine how much filling you need to do, simply measure the front and back rails. Using half the difference between their lengths, measure in from each end of the front rail. Make

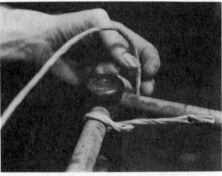

25: Start at left front corner, and tack short strand of rush to side rail. Bring it under front rail; loop over the top and under the side rail, as shown. Then take it under opposite side rail and tack.

26: Second cord is tacked alongside the first and brought across the seat the same way. Tack each of these short cords to the opposite rail. It may take a dozen or so to square off the opening.

pencil marks at these spots. Everything outside these marks must be filled.

The procedure for filling in the corners is clearly shown in photographs 25, 26, and 27. (Directions are given as if you were facing the chair.) Start by tacking one end of a short piece of rush cord inside the left side rail. Bring it under the front rail and then over. Now bring it under the left side rail and over. Then bring the cord across, under the right side rail and over it. Bring it under the front rail next, then over it. Tack the cord to the right side rail directly across from where you tacked it to the left side rail. Cut off the extra cord.

Continue laying these short filler cords until the front rail is covered from the ends to the pencil marks. Remember that each time the rush cord comes over a rail, it crosses all the standing cords before going under the rail at right angles to it.

Now you are ready to weave the first full bout, as shown in figure D. Cut off about 50 feet of rush cord. Some rush weavers use longer strands, but the more you cut off, the more you have to keep pulling through. You will attach the next strand with a square knot, as shown in figure E. Tack one end of the cord to the left side rail, just behind the last filler cord, and weave it just as you did the fillers. But, instead of tacking it to the right side rail, continue through to the back rail and around, looping each corner following the pattern shown in figure D.

Continue weaving around like this for 12 to 15 bouts. As you weave, push each cord tightly against its neighbor where it turns around the rails. Use a block of wood and a small hammer to compact them snugly against each other.

The next step is to stuff the seat. The four triangular pockets must be stuffed separately. You will see the pockets beginning to form between top and bottom layers. Simply stuff newspaper into the corners of each pocket, and continue stuffing as you weave. Or cut four triangles of corrugated cardboard, insert them in the pockets, and weave around them.

Continue weaving until the side rails are completely covered. If the seat is wider than it is deep, the front rails will not be covered yet. Wherever you are at this point, just continue weaving from front to back rail (or vice versa), going between the cross cords in the center, as in figure F. Weave these figure eights across from one side to the other until the front and back rails are filled. Use a block of wood and a hammer to mash cords flat where they cross to fill in better. Bring the cord underneath, and untwist about 4 inches at the end. Apply glue and retwist the cord end into an adjoining cord. To finish the seat, stain it as you wish, and then give it a couple of coats of thin shellac.

27: To square up the seat, fill in the corners with short strands of rush. Tack each strand to the side rails at both ends. When corner areas are full, you can weave one strand around continuously.

28: After four full bouts, the seat looks like this, each strand at right angles to front and back rails. The work moves quickly from now on. If you must stop, clamp the rush to keep it tight.

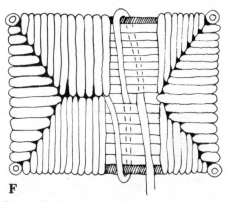

F

Figure F: When a seat is wider than it is deep, side rails will be filled before front and back rails are. Fill in by simply weaving figure eights through the center. Mash the rush flat where it crosses, so it will fill in better.

29: The strands of a well-woven rush seat are laid tightly together. Use a hammer and a block of wood to compact them. Finish the seat with shellac.

RUG BRAIDING
Making New from Old

Michelle Lester is a nationally known weaver and designer. Her handmade rugs, wall hangings, and fiber sculptures have been exhibited throughout the United States and have won numerous awards. She teaches textile design at the Fashion Institute of Technology, in New York City, and the Brooklyn Museum Art School.

Braiding is a simple way to plait fibrous materials into heavy strands, which can then be made into useful household items. Braids of strips from old clothes and remnants were used effectively by Colonial Americans, who fashioned them into oval or circular mats, spiraling the braided strands from a central curl until all available material was used.

In Colonial times, cloth could only be imported from England at exorbitant prices or be handloomed, so valuable worn cloth was reused in many ways. Warm woolen cloth was especially at a premium during the bitter New England winters. When it had provided protection to the struggling pioneers as garments, later cut down for children, and the garments had finally worn out, the heavy, insulating qualities of braided wool cloth, in its final phase, gave warmth underfoot. Lovely color patterns were developed for rugs by combining faded and redyed cloth, and certain color sequences were established and carried on as a folkcraft.

Today a great variety of materials, in many colors and patterns, is readily available, but the concept of recyling outgrown or scrap fabric is still appealing. Used fabrics often contribute softer colors and textures than do new fabrics, and new and used can be combined. Equipment for most braiding projects consists of simple household and sewing tools, although electric scissors and a sewing machine make shorter work of preparing fabric strips. There are even mail-order sources of inexpensive sturdy fabrics and precut strips of woven and knitted goods.

In general, the look of braided things is casual, making them best suited to country settings, recreation areas, and children's rooms, but choices of materials and color influence the final effect, so that unusual braided designs may be used in formal settings. The projects presented here will show how simple it is to make a braided shape, and how to plan practical projects and make unusual designs, using paper patterns.

Preparing Materials

Fabrics of different types may be used together, but combine only those goods in one project that need the same care and are of the same weight. A sewing scrap or purchased remnant usually should be washed before work begins, to test its colorfastness and shrink-resistance, but a used fabric has probably been washed enough to ensure that it will neither run nor shrink. Some fabrics must be dry-cleaned and should be used for something that does not need frequent cleaning.

In choosing colors, lay out the remnants or partly worn clothing available, and decide which colors and textures complement one another. Remember that patterned fabrics will appear speckled in the many twists they will take, so patterns can be combined. I have found, however, that the braids have an especially fresh, crisp look if at least one solid-color strand is included in each combination of three strands.

Fabric weight influences the bulk of each braid and the thickness of the finished product, so similar weights work best together. To be sure your materials are suited to one another and to the project, make short sample braids, following individual project directions. Braid somewhat loosely, as you will in the final work, to allow for spiraling and turning into shapes. If the braid seems too thick, try another sample

1: Braiding projects require scissors, compass, ruler, marking pencil, masking or cellophane tape, needle and pins, carpet thread, iron, C clamp, fabric cut into strips and sewn into long lengths, and, for large projects, metal braid aids.

Taping a contemporary braided rug made of discarded knits is the last step before sewing. The techniques for making this mat are borrowed from the Colonial Americans. Project instructions begin on page 156.

with narrower strips; if too thin, cut wider strips. These experiments will often help you find the proper thickness, but if results are still not satisfactory, try fabric of other weights.

How To Cut

Cut all the clean fabric into strips of proper width. With woven goods, the cuts should be on the bias, or diagonal to the grain of the weave. Fold fabric as in figure A, to establish the proper diagonal: a 45-degree angle. If you are using a garment for strips, cut it first into flat sections, discarding useless collars, cuffs, and any other detailing. Open hems to lie flat. If material is woven, find the thread directions, and cut bias strips as in figure A. When all cloth of one color has been cut into even widths, sew ends of the strips together to make very long pieces, and gently roll the strips into balls of convenient size.

Many knits tend to stretch several ways, so they needn't be cut in any particular direction. Jersey slacks, for instance, could be cut in a gradual spiral down the legs, providing they are seamless or have tiny seams.

Suppliers

If supplies are not available locally, here are a few mail-order sources:

Berry's of Maine, 20-22 Main Street, Yarmouth, Maine 04096 (wools, strip cutters, accessories, heavy threads, books).

The Fabric Shop, Route 53, Pembroke, Mass. 02359 (wools, kits, accessories).

Nu-flex Co., 246 First Avenue South, St. Petersburg, Fl. 33701 (wool strips, kits, accessories).

Tinkler & Co., Inc., P.O. Box 17, Norristown, Pa. 19404 (jersey strips).

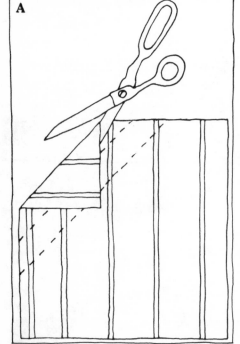

Figure A: Bias cuts follow a 45-degree angle from straight grain (direction of fabric threads) in woven goods. Angle is found by folding material as shown.

2: Place three bias-cut cotton strips with points together. These tapered ends will allow a few narrow beginning twists, which are easier to sew under than blunt ends, especially in making small items.

3: Clamp the three strips tightly to a table or chair back, using a C clamp. Small pieces of cardboard between clamp and furniture will prevent marring it. Or close strips in a drawer to hold them.

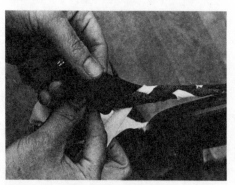

4: The first few twists of braid are made close to points of the strips. Turn the raw edges of the fabric in toward each other just before you twist them. This minimizes fraying of the cloth.

5: Maintain a slight tension to keep the braiding even; but be careful not to pull too tightly, as this would make it difficult to turn the braid into circular form. The braids should be flexible.

6: The first turns of finished braid are made into a tight circle and pinned into place, with the three fabric tips on the wrong side. Begin spiraling, with braid flat and edges touching.

7: With carpet thread, stitch on wrong side, as in this example of a coaster (see below), catching the edge of each round alternately. Ease the braid around the edge as you work so coaster lies flat.

For Deirdre Synek, age 12, braiding a set of four red-white-and-blue coasters to go under her family's iced-tea mugs was a project that required only an afternoon.

8: When coaster is the proper size, trim the ends to points and turn to wrong side. Fan out the points, to prevent bulkiness, and stitch down firmly. Coaster should be even and round.

9: Press the coasters lightly with a steam iron or a dry iron and damp press cloth. Be sure the coasters lie flat, to support glasses firmly. If they don't, cut stitches, and sew again, more loosely.

Braided coasters

To make four coasters, you need about half a square yard of each of three fabrics in your choice of colors. They can be sewing square remnants or material from worn out or outgrown clothing. Absorbent fabrics are best. Cut the material into strips about 1¼ inches wide. Sew them end to end, as explained on the opposite page. For each coaster, you'll need three strands, each about 36 inches long—48 inches long for bigger coasters. Follow the step-by-step procedure given below and as shown in the photographs on this page to make the coasters:

Gather the pointed ends of the three strips, and clamp securely (see photograph 3). Using a three-strand braid, as shown in figure B, begin braiding close to the clamped points. Keep the braid twists loose; pull on the strands only enough to keep braiding even.

Pin both ends of the completed braid temporarily, and begin shaping. Curl one end into a small, tight circle; pin flat, with pointed ends underneath. Lead the braid around this circle, keeping it flat, for one round. Stitch together, catching touching sides of braid alternately and including the points. Ease another round into place; pin if necessary, and stitch. Don't tug the braid; if you do, it won't lie flat. Continue until the work is coaster size. As you work, check for size and roundness—incomplete rounds make a slightly oval shape. Add another round if it is needed. Cut off excess braid, tapering the ends. Turn these points to the underside, and stitch down securely. Press the finished coaster, following directions for photograph 9.

B

Figure B: A three-hand braid consists of three strands. The outer two are turned in alternately to become the center strand. Keep each turn even.

These braided placemats are easy to shape if you tape the braids to a paper guide. Combining plain and patterned sewing scraps makes this an inexpensive project. The placemats are miniatures of the braided oval rugs our grandmothers made.

Braided placemats

The time-honored oval used in braided rugs is an ideal shape for place mats. Simply cut the strips a little narrower to make thinner braids and smaller ovals. Four yards of 36- to 42-inch wide material will give you four mats. Washable fabrics are a practical choice, and plain and patterned fabrics can be combined to complement tableware. The mats at the left were made of checked gingham, plain green and white cottons, and a leafy floral print on a white ground. To complete the mats, you will also need a large sheet of paper, ruler, compass, tape, marking pen, needle, and strong thread.

Make a pattern on the sheet of paper by drawing circles about an inch larger all around than your dinner plates. Photographs 10 and 11 show the steps; figure C diagrams the complete oval pattern. For lightweight fabric such as gingham, cut strips 1½ inches wide; for heavier fabrics, such as poplin, cut strips 1 inch to 1¼ inches wide. (Note: Experts often stitch several different patterns of fabric end to end in each strip.) Now make long braid and begin shaping your mat.

Lay out the design by lightly taping the braids to the paper pattern with the face of the mat against the paper (photograph 12). Use small bits of tape at intervals. When the mat has grown to about 6 inches in width, complete a round; cut the braid, turn points back toward the center of the mat, and tape. Introduce two or three rounds of contrasting braid (photograph 13), and again lay ends toward center and tape. Return to the original coloring for enough rounds to come within an inch from the edge of your pattern. Finish with a few rounds of accent colors.

After the layout is complete, make sure all braid ends are on the surface facing you, and begin to stitch the braids in place, starting at the center. Remove the finished placemat from its paper pattern, and steam press it, or dampen it and press with a warm dry iron. As you press, block the mat into a perfect oval by pulling the edges slightly. If necessary, check its shape against the paper pattern.

Elaine Latham used traditional color sequences in this braided rug, which is made entirely of wool. Instructions for making it are on the opposite page.

◄ 10: Size of placemats depends on the dishes to be used with them. Put a plate face down on drawing paper; center compass (often, plate's center is marked by a tiny dot of glaze), and draw a circle. Allow an inch extra all around.

▼11: With compass set to same radius, use edge of first circle as center for the second. Join the interlocked shapes with straight lines at top and bottom and add a line from center to center.

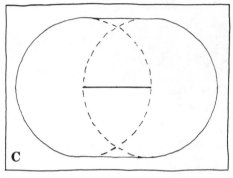

Figure C: Make placemat pattern from two circles about an inch larger all around than a dinner plate. The centers are joined, as are the tops and bottoms.

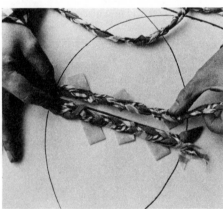

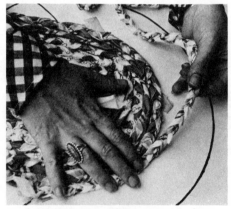

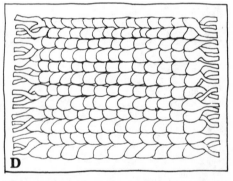

12: Begin by taping first braid above and below center mark. Ease plenty of extra braid into the sharp turns, especially near the mat's center. This prevents the growing oval shape from buckling.

13: As the mat grows, add rounds of new color combinations where they seem desirable. Use bits of tape frequently as sharp curves are shaped. If the work buckles, pull up braid, and lay it again.

Figure D: Another simple placemat shape is a rectangle, with short lengths of braid filling the pattern in parallel rows. The ends can be stitched invisibly.

Traditional braided rug

The traditional oval rug pictured opposite was made by a native New Englander, Elaine Latham. She follows a time-honored formula for coloring the beautifully made rugs that decorate her Early American home. New colors are introduced, one at a time, so that color changes are very gradual. Dark shades at the outside edge make the rug appear flat, and interesting colors at the center focus attention.

Decide dimensions, and subtract the width from the length. The remainder is the length of the starting braid. Use coating wool in 1½- to 2-inch strips. Cut lighter weight wool wider, or tuck an extra strip inside the light one as filler. Allow ¾ of a pound of wool per square foot of rug. Turn in raw edges of strips as you braid. No taping is necessary; sew rounds in place with carpet thread. Tuck in ends, and sew tightly, to make the rug reversible.

Petal-design rug

14: Metal braid aids guide heavy fabrics into neat rolls, with edges tucked in. Aids are especially helpful when you braid heavy fabrics for a rug.

About 9 pounds of cotton-jersey strips were enough to make the petal-design rug below. Cut knit goods yourself, or purchase precut strips, or use woven goods as in previous projects. Choose about 8 pounds of goods in colors that will blend into a predominant tone for the rug. The remainder of the material should provide an accent color for defining the center and border. For rug-making, you may want to purchase small metal cones equipped with tension devices, designed to help heavy strips curl neatly into the braids (see photograph 14). Several brands are available in needlework shops or from the sources listed on page 152.

On a piece of paper 4 feet square, draw a circle 16 inches in diameter, and another 45 inches in diameter, using the same center. To draw large circle, attach a pencil to the end of a string and pivot it around a push pin. Space six radii equally around the circles. Following the steps in figure E, lay braid in the center circle with tape, as described earlier. With main rug color, fill the shape within half an inch of its edge. Next, use the accent braid to outline the circle, and, at the same time, form the dividing shapes that protrude about 6 inches along the radii. To fill in petals, work from the outside of each petal toward the center. The unusual

The unusual petal design of this rug was first planned and shaped on paper. Unique contemporary designs are easy to make with this method.

shape will be easier to fill in this way. You may have to pull up the taped braid at times, to adjust it to fit the difficult turns in the spiral. Keep the braid as flat as possible. The next accent rings must indent deeply between the rounded petals to fill in gaps. As you put the final rounds in place, only a slight indentation is needed. This gives the rug an interesting but practical silhouette. If indentations were too deep, the edges might curl or be caught up under foot. To make the rug reversible, tuck the ends of the braids or colors carefully into neighboring twists and stitch them securely. Figure F shows a method of tucking in ends, and an alternative technique—butting ends together.

Once you have completed one of the braided projects shown here, you may want to design your own. Designs can be adapted from floral motifs or geometric patterns, simplified to suit the braiding technique. Color plays a primary role. Remember that it contributes both hue and value. Hue is the family of the color—red, blue, green. Value is its lightness or darkness. A light blue strand in an otherwise dark braid has an effect much different from a royal or navy blue. Dark blues give the whole braid a darker appearance, and the braid's effect in the total design is a strong, dark line. Light blue, however, will create regular, distinct spots as it twists its way in and out of the braid, making a dotted line in the design. In the same way, a braid of three entirely different values appears even more like a broken line. All these variations can create pleasing effects and are useful in developing patterns.

Broken color lines are good transitional patterns. When you introduce a bold color change, a useful trick is to add the new color first as one part of a preceding round. The traditional formulas for introducing new colors make the transitions even more gradual, as in the rug pictured on page 154.

Unusual materials often suggest projects: rope and twine, nubby silks, raffia, and ribbons may provide inspiration.

Figure E: The five steps in shaping the petal rug are sketched here: Filling the central circle with the main color; adding an accent outline with six spokes to begin petals; filling each petal with the main color from outline toward the center; circling the petals with accent color—indenting to fill gaps between petals; and finishing with smoother rounds of mixed colors. Tape whole plan before sewing.

▶ Figure F: At right are two methods for joining braids in the work: The three ends may be tucked into neighboring braid to make a tapered finish (bottom), or the ends of two meeting braids can be tucked into themselves to make blunt ends, which are then butted together and stitched (top). Tapering must be used for final round.

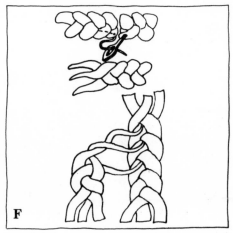

CRAFTNOTES ON ENLARGING PATTERNS

Throughout Colonial Crafts, patterns are reproduced for you to copy. To make a pattern full size, follow the system described here for enlarging the grid imposed on the heart pattern.

The system is really very simple. The small grid in the book must be translated onto a grid with larger squares that you will make; the design (in this case, the heart, for example) will be copied onto this larger grid. The size of the enlarged grid you make will depend on what the pattern is for. A gauge is given with each pattern printed. Draw the squares of the large grid you prepare to the size given by this gauge.

Before you cut your pattern, be sure an allowance has been made for seams.

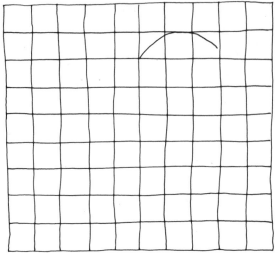

Draw pattern onto your ¼-inch grid a square at a time.

Above is the pattern of a heart. The grid placed over it is divided into small squares that actually measure ⅛ inch. All the patterns in Colonial Crafts use grids of this size. On page 71, the pattern for dolls' clothes is reproduced on such a ⅛-inch grid. To make a pattern that will produce the clothes in the size pictured, you must transfer the pattern onto a grid whose squares are ¼-inch in size, as noted with the pattern.

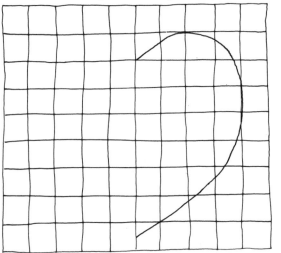

Follow the lines around, checking the book as you go.

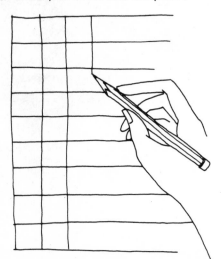

To enlarge the pattern, prepare a grid that has the same number of squares as our illustrated grid for the dolls' clothes, but one in which each square measures ¼-inch on each side.

You will find it easy to transfer the whole pattern.

INDEX